TRILOGY OF RESISTANCE

TRILOGY OF RESISTANCE

ANTONIO NEGRI

Translated by Timothy S. Murphy

Afterword by Barbara Nicolier

UNIVERSITY OF MINNESOTA PRESS
MINNEAPOLIS
LONDON

Published in French in 2009 as *Trilogie de la différence.* Copyright 2009 Éditions Stock.

Published by the University of Minnesota Press
111 Third Avenue South, Suite 290
Minneapolis, MN 55401-2520
http://www.upress.umn.edu

Library of Congress Cataloging-in-Publication Data

Negri, Antonio, 1933–
[Trilogia della resistenza]
Trilogy of resistance / Antonio Negri ; translated by Timothy S. Murphy ; afterword by Barbara Nicolier.
    p. cm.
Includes bibliographical references.
ISBN 978-0-8166-7293-6 (acid-free paper) — ISBN 978-0-8166-7294-3 (pbk. : acid-free paper)
I. Murphy, Timothy S., 1964– II. Title.
PQ4874.E326T7513 2011
852'.914—dc22

                                                                                        2010044066

Printed in the United States of America on acid-free paper

The University of Minnesota is an equal-opportunity educator and employer.

18 17 16 15 14 13 12 11   10 9 8 7 6 5 4 3 2 1

CONTENTS

TRANSLATOR'S NOTE

In order to produce a functional dramatic text of these plays, I had to modify the translations of two of Negri's key philosophical terms that have become standard over the past two decades. The linked Italian terms *potere* and *potenza*, which correspond to the French *pouvoir* and *puissance*, refer respectively to power in an institutionalized, repressive, hierarchical, or transcendent sense and to power in a fluid, creative, constituent, and immanent sense. *Potere/pouvoir* and *potenza/puissance* are normally translated into English as Power and power, often with the Italian or French term included in brackets for clarity. Because the typographical distinction of capitalization is inaudible and the inclusion of bracketed terms is likely to impede the performance of the plays, I simply translated *potere/pouvoir* as "power" and *potenza/puissance* as "potency." Adjectives derived from these nouns are translated accordingly: "powerful," "potent," and so on.

The title of the French volume on which the present translation is based is *Trilogie de la différence* (Éditions Stock, 2009). In discussions after the publication of the French edition, Negri expressed to me a preference for a different English title, *Trilogy of Resistance*, which the publisher has respected.

TRANSLATOR'S INTRODUCTION |
Pedagogy of the Multitude

> The theatre became an affair for philosophers, but only
> for such philosophers as wished not just to explain the
> world but also to change it.
> —Bertolt Brecht, in *Brecht on Theatre: The Development of
> an Aesthetic*

Antonio Negri's militant experiences and critical writings have never
lacked drama in a colloquial sense—political imprisonment, parlia-
mentary elections, and clandestine border crossings, on the one hand,
and panegyrics to anonymous militants, rationalist metaphysicians,
and Roman Catholic saints, on the other, give his career a "marquee
value" that other thinkers simply can't match—but they have rarely
touched on the theater. Indeed, little in his work suggested any interest in drama in the strict sense of writing for theatrical performance,
yet in 2004 his first play, *Swarm*, premiered at the Théâtre de Vidy-
Lausanne in a production directed by Barbara Nicolier that later moved
to the Théâtre National de la Colline in Paris. Two years later, *The Bent
Man* premiered in Viterbo before moving to Rome and Vienna. *Cithaeron* was first staged by students from the Sorbonne at La Colline
in the summer of 2007. In October of that year the same theater staged
dramatic readings of Negri's entire *Trilogy of Resistance*, which were
broadcast on France Culture in 2008. What, if anything, do these plays
have to do with Negri's better-known work in political and ontological

philosophy, especially his influential notions of Empire and multitude? I will argue that Negri's theatrical work is closely related to his philosophical and political work, acting as a pedagogical apparatus intended to engage performers and spectators directly and synchronously, to stage and debate the phenomenological implications of his ideas, and, most importantly, to help produce the common and make the multitude. His dramatic practice is thus an ontological poetics or *poeisis*.

Each of Negri's plays bears a quasi-Brechtian subtitle that makes its pedagogical focus explicit: *Swarm: Didactics of the Militant*, *The Bent Man: Didactics of the Rebel*, and *Cithaeron: Didactics of Exodus*. In Negri's theoretical work these three terms or topoi are particularly important to an understanding and practice of the multitude, the constitutive agent of Negri's political philosophy. For my purposes here, the most important characteristic of the multitude is its mode of activity: the multitude produces the common, which is to say an inclusive community made up of differential singularities rather than an exclusionary one made up of identical individuals, in every form of labor or category of goods we examine. In Hardt and Negri's terms, this production of the common is a feedback spiral between subjectivity and communication: "Subjectivity . . . is produced through cooperation and communication and, in turn, this produced subjectivity itself produces new forms of cooperation and communication, which in turn produce new subjectivity, and so forth."[1] Since sociality is now directly productive, this affirmative spiral operates autonomously, that is, independently of capitalist organization, which in the emerging paradigm of imperial governance no longer serves as the symmetrical/dialectical counterpart of labor power but merely as an antagonistic apparatus of capture defined by its expropriation of the common.[2] Hardt and Negri further distinguish between the multitude *sub specie aeternitatis*, the ontological multitude or multitude "in itself" without which "we could not conceive our social being," and the political or historical multitude, the "not-yet multitude" or multitude "for itself" that is both subject and object of their theoretical project.[3] Revolutionary political action in the present depends on making the latter out of the former. Like the common, we must make or produce the multitude for itself theoretically, organizationally, and, of course, politically, but also poetically or theatrically. But how?

If the value of both *Empire* and *Multitude* lies in the large-scale cognitive map that these texts construct of the emerging global order, as I have argued elsewhere,[4] then Negri's plays work like the zoom tools that online maps have taught us to use: they enlarge certain local conditions of subjectivation and struggle to the point of discernibility and thereby make them available for practical experimentation. In this the plays resemble the italicized excurses included in *Empire* and *Multitude,* which often illuminate the interstices of the imperial order by poetic means. Both the large-scale and the close-up maps must be understood in Deleuze and Guattari's sense of the term: a map, they write, is "an experimentation in contact with the real . . . open and connectable in all of its dimensions . . . detachable, reversible, susceptible to constant modification . . . [which] can be torn, reversed, adapted to any kind of mounting, reworked by an individual, group or social formation."[5] Such maps are valuable less for their objective precision than for the kinds of experimentation they make possible, and following one is an exercise in a kind of production or creation that we might call poetic. This aspect of their work is what leads critics like William Smith Wilson and Joseph Tabbi to describe Hardt and Negri's books as "world-poems" or "world-fictions."[6] Extending this line of argument, then, Negri's dramas could be described as world-plays.

If we take their didactic subtitles seriously, we must recognize that Negri's plays are (related to) *Lehrstücke* or "learning plays," perhaps Bertolt Brecht's most radical innovation in drama, that are designed to educate their performers as much as their audiences:

> The *Lehrstück* teaches by being played, not by being seen. In principle, spectators are not needed for the *Lehrstück,* although they can of course be utilized. It is basic to the *Lehrstück* that the people playing can be socially influenced by the execution of certain attitudes, the adoption of certain postures, the repetition of certain speeches, and so forth. In this regard, the imitation of highly viable patterns plays a large role, as does the criticism of those patterns, which will be carried out through well-considered, altered modes of playing.[7]

Brecht sometimes described these learning plays as "meetings," and Hanns Eisler called them "political seminars," but they seem to go beyond the traditional discussion/debate model of the meeting or seminar because one learns with one's body as well as one's mind, by

adopting the postures, performing the actions, and making the state-
ments characteristic of different kinds of subjects. Fredric Jameson, following the lead of Brecht scholar Reiner Steinweg, calls them "master
classes," meaning by that a situation of "infinite rehearsals, in which,
in true Brechtian fashion, all the alternatives can be tried out in turn
and endlessly debated. Meanwhile, the passage of the various actors
through all the roles necessarily creates a multidimensionality which
is the very essence . . . of theater itself."[8] Barbara Nicolier's staging of
Negri's plays has, to a certain extent, followed this multidimensional
model.

Essentially, a learning play teaches—without anyone taking the role
of teacher—by staging the adoption of different social subject positions
by the actors; roles are performed in the epic style, which estranges
the actor from the role at the same time that it distances the spectator
from the process of identification. Here, "staging" (which is also the
word Marx uses, in German *aufführen*, at the start of the *Eighteenth
Brumaire* to characterize the displacement that allows a revolution to
be carried out)[9] means something more than the mise en scène, something closer to Jameson's explication of the master-class conception of
the learning play:

> one feature it makes clear is the inseparable presence of so-called *theory*
> within the larger "text" itself. It is not that the theory becomes a work
> of art in its own right, nor does the artistic text simply reincorporate the
> theory and become a new kind of collage or experiment in "mixed media."
> Rather, theorizing . . . is part of the process itself, and you could just as
> easily claim that the original play or text exists in order to provoke the
> theory and give it content, occasion and raw material as, more convention-
> ally, that the theory is simply there to guide a more fitting production of
> the text.[10]

Jameson is referring to Brecht's dramatic theory and its relation to
his plays, but I would argue that a similar reciprocal process occurs
between Negri's plays and his political and ontological theory, and that
this mode of theatrical production constitutes a very specific production of the common—the feedback spiral between theory and play not
only manifests the fundamental spiral of communication and subjectivity but also explicates it, maps it, and puts its logic on display as both
a provocation and an invitation to experiment through language.

Hardt and Negri's emphasis on communication has most often been analyzed by reference to digital media and communications technology, but those modes are ultimately predicated on the characteristics of natural languages, especially their figurative capacities. Drawing on Paolo Virno's work at the juncture of linguistic and economic production, Hardt and Negri insist upon "the triple relation to the common: our power to speak is based in the common, that is, our shared language; every linguistic act creates the common; and the act of speech itself is conducted in common, in dialogue, in communication."[11] The centrality of dialogue already invokes an element of theatricality, but they theorize the production of the common in terms that bring it even closer to theater (and to Brecht's learning play) when, following Judith Butler, they identify "the conceptual shift from *habit* to *performance* as the core notion of the production of the common . . . Performance, like habit, involves neither fixed immutable nature nor spontaneous individual freedom, residing instead between the two, a kind of acting in common based on collaboration and communication."[12] Like Butler's, this conception is not limited to stage performance—as Hardt and Negri point out, "Every form of labor that produces an immaterial good . . . is fundamentally a performance: the product is the act itself"[13]—but it may tentatively be described as a constitutive ontologization of theatricality.

Negri overtly situates his plays in a Brechtian line of theatrical development: scene C2[14] of *Swarm* contains a brief allusion to *Mother Courage* as well as a citation from *Der Auftrag* (*The Task* or *The Mission*) by Heiner Müller, perhaps Brecht's most controversial theatrical heir (as well as an acquaintance of Negri's through their mutual friend Félix Guattari).[15] These two playwrights provide a formal and political frame of reference for Negri's didactic dramas; as he has written, "there is more than one didactics: Brecht's lashes the conscience in Enlightenment fashion, while Müller's tortures bodies—the inevitable consequence of a didactic estrangement that finds itself faced with a society of bodies traumatized by capital."[16] Indeed, Negri describes Müller's theater as part of his own privileged countertradition of modernity:

> Müller's didactics is ethical, remains communist and continues to produce adequate effects . . . Ethics in Spinoza is the very fabric of life that is traversed and transformed by the passion of the eternal. But the eternal is the common . . . On this stage [Spinoza's] ethics develops into Müller's

didactics—within a present that permits no escape, within a common that is shrouded in drama. Here the eternal is open to an always irresistible act of critique and refusal.[17]

This is precisely the act to which Negri's own theater—and philosophy—aspires. But Negri also cautions that "the reference to Brecht and Müller is as important as it is critical . . . The theme of this theater of mine is really the discovery of a 'new' militancy that is difficult to relate to Brecht's 'old' militancy and/or the critical (or self-critical) militancy of Müller."[18]

Perhaps the most important focus of Negri's didactics in *Trilogy of Resistance* is the problem of the relationship between the multitude's production of the common and violence. The plays interrogate many modes of violence and ultimately struggle to stage what Hardt and Negri call "democratic violence."[19] The focus on violence is no surprise, because Negri has wrestled with this problem often in his writings and in his activist/organizational work. In *Swarm*, the protagonist is pushed to the brink of violence by her savage indignation over the suffering of the world.[20] She imagines assuming a series of militant roles that are defined by the forms of violence specific to them: the solitary suicide bomber driven by hatred to use her body as a weapon against power (A2–A3); the party member compelled by ideology to subordinate her singularity to the demands of normative class consciousness, to fight, kill, and die on the orders of the party leadership (C2–C3); finally, in the closing scenes, the protagonist discovers the swarm as a form of collectivity that expresses and defends singularities, a "cloud in the form of a sword" (D2) that fights a rearguard, defensive action against the armies that would block the exodus of the multitude from Empire. *The Bent Man*, a "war story," further develops the critique of violence by dramatizing the struggle of an Italian woodcutter who resists fascism by bending himself double to avoid military conscription, but who must later commit a monumental act of defensive violence, one that takes his own life, in order to defend his common—he must make "war on war . . . with the soul and the body, singularly and in common" (III Elegy).[21] Finally, in *Cithaeron*, which rewrites Euripides' *Bacchae*, the ruling family of Thebes, like the city itself, is literally torn apart and reconstructed in the course of its encounter with the forces of living labor, personified in the "human god" Dionysus, who is portrayed as a "young man from the suburbs" (I.C) (presumably the ghetto suburbs of Paris, not the upscale suburbs of London or Los Angeles). Negri reinterprets the dismemberment of the tyrant Pentheus by his mother Agaue, which is traditionally viewed as an unforgivable moral abomination, instead as an adequate figure for the responsive democratic violence of the revolutionary process.

What even these brief summaries suggest is that Negri's plays explicitly attempt to stage—in that expanded sense of the learning play as master class—a reconceptualization of the most basic elements of political philosophy; if *Empire* and *Multitude* produce political philosophy poetically, then the plays do so dramatically. The terms of this reconceptualization have been widely recognized and debated. The resisting subject can no longer find an open space or a normative form in which to amplify and aggregate its militancy. Exodus can no longer seek a place outside Empire, because nowhere is outside Empire. "Whereas being-against in modernity often meant a direct and/or dialectical opposition of forces, in postmodernity being-against might well be most effective in an oblique or diagonal stance. Battles against the Empire might be won through subtraction and desertion. This desertion does not have a place; it is the evacuation of the places of power."[22] Now that it has become permanent and biopolitical, war can no longer be defined as an external relation between states, and defensive violence can no longer operate outside the general horizon of war—it must function within that horizon. "The exodus and emergence of democracy is thus a war against war . . . A *democratic* use of force and violence is neither the same as nor the opposite of the war of sovereignty: it is different."[23] All these negative definitions point in the same direction, which is the direction in which Negri's plays—and his philosophy—are aiming: they intend to displace both discourse and action from extension to intensity. If the individual subject is immediately subsumed into imperial circuits that expropriate its communicative, rational, and affective performances, then resistance must produce intensive difference or singularity within subjective forms. If war is a permanent background to imperial sociality, then defensive violence must express its intensive difference within war itself. And exodus must lead to an elsewhere that is within—but against—Empire.

I noted earlier that little in Negri's earlier work suggests any interest in theater—little, but not nothing. There are a few important clues scattered throughout his writings that, in retrospect, should reduce the surprise his readers may feel at this development. Most significant to my mind is his tendency to adopt rhetorical personae in his theoretical writings, to ventriloquize and thereby valorize different subject positions. Probably the most famous—and unsettling—example of this is his adoption of the persona of a clandestine militant in his pamphlet *Domination and Sabotage* (1977).

> I am therefore within this separation that connects me to the world as a force of destruction. I am within it and I feel the intensity of the leap of change that is presupposed every time that I free myself through destruction . . . Nothing reveals the immense historical positivity of workers' self-valorization more completely than sabotage, this continual activity of the sniper, the saboteur, the absentee, the deviant, the criminal that I find myself living. I immediately feel the warmth of the workers' and proletarian community again every time I don the ski mask. This solitude of mine is creative, and this separateness of mine is the only real collectivity that I know. Nor does the happiness of the result escape me: every act of destruction and sabotage redounds upon me as a sign of class fellowship . . . Nor does the suffering of the adversary affect me: proletarian justice has the very same productive force of self-valorization and the very same faculty of logical conviction.[24]

This particular case of ventriloquism had far-reaching consequences: it was cited in the warrants authorizing Negri's arrest on April 7, 1979, on charges of murder, kidnapping, membership in an armed band, and insurrection against the powers of the state, and it was later repeated endlessly in Italian media coverage of the April 7 case. It is still cited by right-wing commentators bent on discrediting Negri's contributions to the contemporary debate over globalization.[25]

I cite this passage at length because it reveals Negri's drama to be not only a pedagogy of the multitude but also a self-critique of his own militant experience, particularly his theorization of violence. *Swarm* is in part a rewriting of or counterstatement to the ski-mask passage, an attempt to debate, clarify, and correct its implications and thereby transform his long-standing meditation on violence through an engagement with the present—and thus a good example of the reciprocity between theory and drama that characterizes the learning

play. Formally, *Swarm* is both pre-Aeschylean—meaning that its cast
consists of a protagonist and a chorus, for, as Aristotle tells us, "The
number of actors was first increased to two by Aeschylus, who cur-
tailed the business of the chorus, and made the dialogue . . . take the
leading part in the play"[26]—and for that same reason (post-)Brechtian.
It explicitly addresses Brecht's most controversial learning play, *Die
Massnahme* (*The Measures Taken*), as well as Müller's extension and critique of Brecht in plays like *Mauser*. Like Negri's play, both Brecht's
and Müller's dramatize inquiries, carried out by choruses representing revolutionary groups, into ethically troubling instances of revolutionary violence: in Brecht, the investigation involves the killing by a
group of revolutionary agitators of their comrade whose tactical mis-
takes threaten their mission,[27] while in Müller the inquiry focuses on a
revolutionary executioner whose excessive zeal for his work threatens
his party and results in his own execution.[28] All three plays conclude
with an ethical judgment, that is, a sovereign decision.

   Throughout *Swarm* the protagonist speaks primarily of and to herself, but she also interacts with a chorus that amplifies, undermines, and
contradicts her adoptions and assessments of a series of subject-forms.[29]
Both the protagonist and the chorus try on different roles correspond-
ing to different models of militancy, very much in the way that Brecht's
learning plays in general—and specifically *Die Massnahme*—operate.
Following a prologue expressing the indignation that "shatters the singular continuity of desire, sends it back to us in pieces" (**AI**) and thereby
motivates militancy, the protagonist wallows in a hatred that mirrors
the contempt imperial power feels for its subordinates, and so she first
takes on the role of the suicide bomber, donning a costume armored
with explosives. At the height of the scene she exults, "They call me
terrorist, suicide bomber, assassin. So, what. To die, yes, but dreaming of the groans of a massacred enemy, the terrified screams of those
I will have wounded and mutilated . . ." (**A3**). Note that the language
here parallels that of the ski-mask passage quoted earlier. Although
motivated by a quasi-dialectical negativity, this asymmetrical mode
of attack cannot defeat the massed violence of imperial power—the
chorus pointedly asks, "If your hatred provokes the enemy, isn't that
because it resembles him even before it has managed to express itself,
and thus it provokes in advance a still more violent reaction?" (**A2**)—nor
does it contribute to the production of the common of resistance: the

chorus warns, "Don't imagine that you are the expression of a world, a generation . . . You are alone" (A2). The debate staged here ultimately refutes the ski-mask passage, even to the point of reversing its controlling metaphor of militant disguise: the protagonist of *Swarm* removes her explosive-laden clothes to contemplate the naked flesh, the life she shares with the multitude, "the common of multiplicity" (B2); she then re-dresses in "the clothes of others, men and women, young and old, white and black" to become "the potent harlequin" (CI) of the multitude (an image that will recur in *Cithaeron*'s depiction of Dionysus "adorning [him]self in increasingly artificial and appealing ways" [II.C]).

The next seduction comes from totalizing ideology, Müller's Angel of Despair, "a knowledge only for the few . . . that claims to contain everything in itself and to bring the passion of the great many to fruition in its totality" (C2), and ideology's self-proclaimed agency of transcendence, the party: "Nothing is possible when one is alone, only the party can make us effective, all together we advance holding hands . . . When you belong to the corps of revolutionaries, you must be ready to die and kill for the revolution!" (C3). Initially, the protagonist sings along with the marching Red Army Chorus into which the dramatic chorus has been molded, but both soon see through the restrictive illusions: "Singularity no longer has any need of totality, it rises up against death" (C3). Both the party's claim to represent the subjects it subsumes and its claim to a monopoly on violence, which strictly parallel the claims of the state and which Müller (if not Brecht) subjects to ironic scrutiny, must be dismantled. These scenes effectively recapitulate the critique of the party-form over which Negri vacillated for years during the 1970s, and which culminates in the new definition of militancy offered in *Empire:*

> Today the militant cannot even pretend to be a *representative,* even of the fundamental human needs of the exploited. Revolutionary political militancy today, on the contrary, must rediscover what has always been its proper form: *not representational but constituent activity.* Militancy today is a positive, constructive, and innovative activity . . . Militants resist imperial command in a creative way. In other words, resistance is linked immediately . . . to the formation of cooperative apparatuses of production and community . . . It knows only an inside, a vital and ineluctable participation in the set of social structures, with no possibility of transcending them.[30]

Having critiqued and abandoned suicidal escapism and the transcendence of the party, the protagonist must turn to the "cooperative apparatuses of production and community" inside which she has unknowingly lived—the immanence of the multitude.

The protagonist is ultimately led to the swarm, "the common of the multitude" or "the form of collective singularity and subjectivity" that constitutes the multitude's mode of militant organization and network resistance. At this point the chorus breaks up into its component singularities, each speaking its own line to the collective and in the process creating a linguistic polyphony. As the protagonist says, "If there is something like a collective today, this is because it constructs itself by looking into itself . . . the collective gaze into itself is the common of the swarm. No origin, no principle—but a proliferation, a coming and going, an arabesque that develops the order of singularities into ever more radical and contiguous forms of being-together" (D1). The logic of the swarm is largely derived from artificial intelligence, but, as Hardt and Negri acknowledge, it also owes something to Rimbaud's poetic descriptions of the Communards as swarming ants.[31] Nevertheless, the question remains: if the swarm is a "cloud in the form of a sword . . . who is there to wield the sword? Who decides," if not the isolated martyr or the party leaders? The answer the protagonist provides is telling: "The decision . . . is when the multitude begins to produce. I feel the decision like an unexpected leap of being, like a rupture in the repetition of the past, like an unforeseen and yet hoped-for future. The decision is the event, this metamorphosis not only of nature but of time . . ." (D2). The production of the common is itself the decision, the inalienable sovereign right—or, in Spinozist terms, power—of the multitude. As Hardt and Negri note, "The economic [and linguistic/dramatic—TM] production of the multitude . . . is not only a *model* for political decision-making but also tends itself to *become* political decision-making."[32] The play concludes with the swarm's exodus from imperial power, described in terms of the Israelites' flight from Egypt just as it is near the conclusion of *Multitude:*[33] "Defend us, Aaron, prevent the beast from crushing us until the impossible is ultimately produced and the sea finally parts" (D3).

Also near the end of *Multitude,* Hardt and Negri distinguish two concepts of martyrdom, which the protagonist and the chorus of *Swarm* debate and between which they have had to choose:

> The one form, which is exemplified by the suicide bomber, poses martyr-
> dom as a response of destruction, including self-destruction, to an act of
> injustice . . . In [the other] form the martyr does not seek destruction but
> is rather struck down by the violence of the powerful. Martyrdom in this
> form is really a kind of *testimony*—testimony not so much to the injustices
> of power but to the possibility of a new world, an alternative not to that
> destructive power but to every such power . . . This martyrdom is really
> an act of love; a constituent act aimed at the future and against the sover-
> eignty of the present . . . That martyrdom is . . . only a by-product of real
> political action . . .[34]

The protagonist's interrogation, both by the chorus and by herself,
struggles to flesh out this opposition and refine it, making a genuine choice possible. Indeed, the interrogation performs the choice and
makes the decision. Her inquiry ultimately not only distinguishes
between solitary, intentional self-destruction and common resistance,
but it also suggests criteria for distinguishing repressive collectives like
the party-form from expressive or constructive ones like the swarm
and the multitude. Thus, on the conceptual as well as the formal level,
Swarm can be read as a mirror dialogue in which Negri interrogates
himself and the development of his own militancy.[35]

The second form of martyrdom, martyrdom as testimony to a new
world, is the focus of Negri's second play, *The Bent Man*, which is also
a more conventional drama, at least in plot, than *Swarm* (despite its
intertextual allusions to Samuel Beckett's *Endgame*). Following a
choral prologue that addresses the audience directly, the play stages
the quasi-expressionist "war story" of a woodcutter's resistance to the
overwhelming power of the Italian fascist state. Recognizing that he
could not survive an act of open rebellion against the state, he chooses
instead to rebel by withdrawing from its compulsory service: "The fascists always say: I break, but I don't bend. As for me, I bend in order
not to break" (I.B). He draws his strength and his imagery from nature
in order to make himself a new nature, a doubled nature: "when they
come looking for me, I will bend myself double, I will be like a tree
stubbornly twisted to the order of destruction, a twisted tree that stops
the violence of the winds and the storms" (I.A). He recognizes that this
will entail tremendous suffering, but he proclaims that "I am ready to
suffer in order to fool them, to nourish my hatred in silence, to martyr
my body in order to sabotage their war, and to submit to their control in

order to destroy their discipline and infringe their laws" (I.B). Thereby he survives imprisonment and the efforts of doctors, priests, and other fascist collaborators to straighten him up so that he can serve the state and its church. To the priest, who encourages him to join the "just war in defense of religion" and the "holy war . . . against socialism," he responds, "Christ congratulated me because I have a body that is more capable than his of bearing the cross . . . the bent body feels truer than the straight body . . . Christ is holier than God, the cross is not high but low and curved toward the earth" (II.B). This vision of an earthly, militant Christ foreshadows Dionysus, the immanent divinity of *Cithaeron*.

Freed after the fall of Mussolini's government, the woodcutter organizes the struggle against the regrouping fascists and faces the ethical dilemma of rebel violence: "Defending oneself against war does not mean making war . . . Refusing to kill cannot imply having to kill" (III.B). Only when he finds a natural parallel to his original act of doubling himself up does he resolve his conundrum and reconceive his ethics: "Only nature has the right to cause death . . . An avalanche, a disaster, a mountain's vengeance . . . [but] we are a potency of nature . . . We will say no to their will to death, we will show them the complicity that ties us to nature" (III.C). He ultimately dies in the act of "bending" the mountain that overlooks his village down onto the enemy by setting off a cache of mining explosives; this causes a massive landslide, thereby "transform[ing] our landscape into a weapon of war." By bending himself double he made a new self, a second self to resist fascism, and by bending the mountain he makes a second nature, what Negri has described as "nature to the second power," to overcome it—which is possible because human activity is not opposed to an immutable nature but rather acts within nature to transform and renew it, producing it as part of the common. The woodcutter wonders, "What will the eagles and sparrows do when the mountain blows up? Will they feel freer? They will take wing, frightened at first; then nature will seem totally new to them in the midst of the ruins" (III.C). His surviving friends celebrate this bending or redoubling of nature: "The new landscape in which we live is the work of that Man who knew how to make Nature a friend" (Elegy). His death is not a suicide—he struggles to escape from the mineshaft in which the explosives detonate—and it emphatically bears witness to the possibility of a new world: as he tells himself, "We must rebel in this world by constructing another, a new one, within it . . . I'm not happy to act as a witness, but it must be done" (III.C). All his actions throughout the play are motivated by love—for the forests where he labors, for his wife and unborn child, for his fellow prisoners and the villagers who share his resistance to fascism—and he is only reluctantly persuaded to "declare war on war" by the necessity of defending their common. As Hardt and Negri write, "Democratic violence does not initiate the revolutionary process but rather comes only at the end, when the political and social transformation has already taken place, to defend its accomplishments," and thus has nothing to do with the statist theory of just war, which is merely "aggression . . . justified on a moral foundation."[36] The accomplishments of the revolutionary process, of course, constitute the common.

The final play of the trilogy, *Cithaeron*, appears at first glance to be a straightforwardly postmodern type of drama: a pastiche of Euripides' *Bacchae* transposed onto the Internet. Negri's text incorporates all the characters and almost two hundred lines verbatim from Euripides. Yet this appearance is deceptive: Negri's intention is not to de-historicize or deconstruct Euripides' play, but rather to revise and reinterpret it, to open it up to debate, particularly the roles of the god Dionysus and Agaue, the mother of the tyrant Pentheus. In the original Greek tragedy, Agaue goes mad when she realizes that she has killed her son, the King of Thebes, under the influence of Dionysus's intoxicating rituals of worship, and her fate as an infanticide and regicide is traditionally interpreted as a stern warning against denying the god's divinity. Negri seeks to defend her against this interpretation, and in the process develop a more compelling account of defensive or democratic violence than he did in *The Bent Man*. The anonymous voices that introduce the play ask the question right at the start: "How could we ever understand a mother, Agaue, killing her own son? And how can we show that this wasn't a mad and unjustifiable act but a strong affirmation of freedom?" (Parodos). Near the end of *Cithaeron* Dionysus insists that

> What we must understand and recount is not how resistance is transformed into violence, but why . . . The terror undergone, the fear fed by clandestinity, the lacerating decision to resist authority—all that suffering was let go, joy got the upper hand over resentment and dissolved the sad passions that haunted the revolt; and the impression of having done a just thing was generalized—because the regicidal act was seen for what it was: the love of freedom against tyranny. (III.B)

If his rewriting of Euripides is successful, it will demonstrate why, in Negri's view, the play "speaks of us [today], of the way in which a world dominated by a tyrant can be revolutionized by the mobile presence of migrants, by the revolt of women against patriarchy, by the desire for freedom of living labor" (Parodos).

The play is doubly framed, first by a traditional Greek *parodos* that introduces the quasi chorus of voices whose sole purpose is to pose the play's central problem of violence, and second by a twenty-first-century prologue in which a young mixed-race woman encounters the Greek story for the first time and relates it directly to her own situation.[37] She describes Dionysus as "A god capable of new technologies of life and communication . . . capable of arousing enthusiasm and solidarity never before seen—those that the new knowledges put into practice . . . a demonic god": in short, the Dionysus whose labor is celebrated in Hardt and Negri's first collaboration, where they describe him as "the god of living labor, creation on its own time, [and the] powers of the netherworld" invoked in the *Communist Manifesto*.[38] But this Dionysus, the mixed-race man of the ghetto, is a god of immanence, not transcendence: the choral voices insist that "if we want to speak of the divine, let's state right away that it resides in us" (Parodos). The young woman sees the mountain Cithaeron, where Agaue and the bacchants hold their festival and which gives the play its title, as "A second nature . . . Traversed by the flows of communication that render any claim to power chaotic." She wants to enter that world, which is also a version of her own; she implores Dionysus to "Take on human form once again, enter into the community of the network to which I belong, free my potency, free our potency," and asks, "How can this savage network in which I am a prisoner be transformed into a free and strong Cithaeron?" (Prologue).

Within the main body of the play it is Agaue who most concretely articulates the project of Dionysian labor when she chastises her father Cadmus and the blind seer Tiresias:

> Dionysus certainly drives us to transgress, but on the condition that we do so in the world of know-how—and that's why we honor him. Today like yesterday—and probably tomorrow too—we accuse the god of impiety because he dares incite us to know. The impious thing is the Enlightenment spirit of Dionysus—not his tragic madness but his logical fury, not his enthusiasm but his will to truth. We expect a serene Socratic philosophy

from him, an effective *technē*, and the industrious construction of a second nature. And Cithaeron is there to embody that project of reason. (I.A)

From the start of Negri's revision, Agaue recognizes her son Pentheus as the greatest threat to the Dionysian spirit of inclusive difference and transgressive knowledge that brought Thebes to its flowering. He denounces the bacchants' claim "that wisdom and the concept are born of a common agreement of citizens, which transforms nature and strives to create a new nature" (I.B).

The confrontations between Pentheus and Dionysus develop this theme further, to the point that Dionysus effectively replaces Pentheus as Agaue's son—she addresses him as such in II.A, and he reciprocates, calling her "my dear mother." This revision of kinship relations foreshadows the play's conclusion, as we will see. Dionysus articulates and extends the conception of defensive democratic violence that emerged at the end of *The Bent Man* when he insists that "You cannot call 'war' the desire to resist injustice, or this knowledge that revolutionizes *technē*, or even the fact that women are affirming their difference within equality," as Pentheus tries to do. Dionysus warns Pentheus that "Revolt is always followed by vengeance—because if love has organized a violence capable of redeeming subjects from repression, once this violence emerges from the cave in which it was confined, it continues to work among men" (II.B). He invites Pentheus to visit Cithaeron and see for himself the "different idea of measure, and justice, and power itself" that the rebels have, to "enter into the game and imagine [he is] the multitude" (II.C). Their arrival on the mountain, in Negri's conceit, takes place across competing Web sites representing the King of Thebes, Agaue, and Dionysus; as in Euripides, Pentheus's death at his mother's hands is not shown but described. At the moment of the killing and after, Agaue is unable to say why she must kill her son—she says that "Dionysus guides me—god is serenely being made man—[but] Dionysus himself would not know how to answer this question" (III.A).

Yet Dionysus offers an answer, one that rebuts the interpretive consensus that surrounds Euripides' play: "They wanted to read into this fable feelings of guilt instead of the joy of an experiment. A mother killed her son! No! A mother killed a tyrant!" (III.B). This is why resistance must sometimes be transformed into violence: it must overcome the ingrained habits of both insurgents and their foes, including the most conventional ethical values, in order to defend the new common that has been produced. In *The Bent Man* the woodcutter's unborn child is the ultimate symbol of the common that must be defended, but in *Cithaeron* the parent–child relation is denaturalized, redoubled, and displaced by the rebel–tyrant relation—and, surprisingly, in inverted form, with the child taking the role of tyrant. Tyrannical violence does not answer to the familial obligation, so it must be met with contrary but democratic violence that also exceeds familial bonds. When Agaue laments that "God will not forgive me," Dionysus responds that "no god can forgive you—because no god exists who is outside our passions . . . What do you want a god to be, if not this desire for freedom that is inside every one of us?" (III.B). She comes to recognize that the pain Pentheus inflicted upon Thebes exceeded the citizens' capacity to endure, and "Once pain has surpassed all measure, vengeance, which we have nevertheless excluded from the order of private rights, reappears despite everything as a thirst for justice." Indeed, she reminds Cadmus that "it was justifiably on the basis of this burning mixture of freedom and terror, pain and chaos that you set your constituent power to work" in the original founding of Thebes (III.C). All the insurgents have done is to reactivate that constituent power to subvert and reconstruct the formal and material constitution of the city.

The play concludes with the young woman of the prologue meeting blind Tiresias on the stage as he leads "those who can see" into exile or exodus—because "in eras of transition . . . imagination alone allows us to advance on a path made of void" (Exodus). The void of which he speaks is what remains after the evacuation of the places of imperial power, which is what the dismemberment of Pentheus has accomplished: the death of the tyrant, but also the critique of the ethical system and form of kinship that guaranteed his power. Here the common is constructed as an elective affinity, immanently produced through the multitude's performance, and arrayed against the transcendence of descent, which is held as an inherited property. The operation of democratic violence here, as in *The Bent Man*, seems to complicate the logical pattern that Hardt identified in Negri's earlier critical work:[39] a *pars destruens* (or destructive step) involving a critique of or break with tradition and habit leads to the *pars construens* (or constructive step) of producing a new common, which must then be followed by a second destructive step of defending that common against constituted power. In any case, this almost dialectical dance of constitution and destruction, resistance and violence appears to be the only possibility for exodus in a world with no outside.

The conclusion of the trilogy raises difficult questions: Can we accept the notion of decision as economic and linguistic production that concludes *Swarm*? If network production is already sovereign in itself, how can it successfully displace imperial sovereignty and become sovereign for itself? Is it already doing so? Can we accept the notion of a redoubled nature that justifies democratic violence in *The Bent Man*? How can this violence be distinguished from the imperial naturalization of overwhelming force as humanitarian intervention, or from the old social Darwinist apology for plutocratic violence? Can we accept the notion that this democratic violence is constitutive of exodus, as *Cithaeron* argues, and that a liberated future can emerge from it? Negri's plays stage these questions but offer no definitive answers. Nevertheless, the concepts produced for and as the common are perhaps less important than the process that produces them, which in Negri's plays may accurately be called theatrical production, a theater for the production of the common.

Negri's plays are designed to provoke discussion and debate around the fundamental questions they raise; they call upon the theoretical intelligence of performers and spectators as well as their poetic sensibilities and affective sympathies. Like Brecht's and Müller's plays, they are likely to strike some viewers as rough-hewn, argumentative, or discordant. But they succeed in staging a significant part of the fractious ongoing dialogue—or polylogue—that constitutes militant activity today, after the collapse of every universal model of resistance. They enact a reciprocal intensification and displacement of the relationship between theory and drama of the sort that Deleuze might have called a relay: theory intervenes to break through the blockages or impasses of drama, and correlatively, drama intervenes to break through the blockages of theory.[40] They consciously aspire to embody a polyphonic narrative and arouse a polyphonic response:

> In a polyphonic conception of narrative there is no center that dictates meaning, but rather meaning arises only out of the exchanges among all the singularities in dialogue. Singularities all express themselves freely and together through their dialogues create the common narrative structures. [Such] polyphonic narrative, in other words, poses in linguistic

terms a notion of the production of the common in an open, distributed network.[41]

Negri's dramatic voice is only one theme in this polyphony, which makes itself heard not by drowning out other voices but by drawing them into a proliferating network, as his philosophical and militant voices have for the past forty years. He doesn't always harmonize fully with his comrades, or even with himself, but classical harmony is neither the method nor the goal. Negri's poetics in no way rely on a Kantian aesthetics of the beautiful. Instead, something closer to the second-order harmony or discordant accord, as well as the immeasurability, of Kant's sublime is at stake here, though without the transcendental illusion in which Kant foreclosed his analysis. Immanence, on the other hand, means self-constitution, self-valorization, self-dramatization without a transcendent guarantee or stabilizing center. The multitude is pure immanence, to speak like Deleuze, because, as Hardt and Negri note,

> the multitude is organized something like a language. All the elements of a language are defined by their differences from the others, and yet they function together . . . A specific expression, then, is not only the combination of linguistic elements but the production of real meanings: expression gives a name to an event. Just as expression emerges from language, then, a decision emerges from the multitude in such a way as to give meaning to the whole and name an event . . . [T]he multitude is itself an active subject—something like a language that can express itself.[42]

To which we can add: something like a drama that can stage itself.

TRILOGY OF RESISTANCE

PREFACE |

Trilogy of Resistance is an object with several facets. Above all I wanted to take up the communist tradition of the epic theater again and try to restore its image for the postmodern era: the project of social transformation—and the transformation of existence itself—could not have the same conditions in the present as in the past. I also sought to make this *Trilogy* an offering of the breath of resistance and the desire for change to different subjects. In *Swarm*, the "Man" embodies a singularity that gradually makes itself into the multitude; in *The Bent Man*, a woodcutter recognizes the otherness that surrounds him and forms the basis of his own revolt; lastly, in *Cithaeron*, the painful and powerful action of constituent justice gradually emerges.

The militant, the rebel, and the migrant: three figures to tell these three stories. Three possibilities of embodying struggle and a life's choices at the same time. Three attempts, finally, to invent a philosophical dramaturgy that is open to the political, a theatrical dialogue able to speak of resistance, doubts, choices, necessities, pain, but also the desire to live—together, with less suffering. Within largely unknown political spaces that are simultaneously terrible and ultimately quite anonymous—spaces traversed by singular lives and open to the experience of each of us—I wanted to take up once again an ancient tradition.

I would like for all this to represent, if only in a small way, a theater of the future perfect. Three theatrical fables, yes, but also three rough drafts of a program for a resisting and desiring life.

A.N.

Swarm premiered at the Théâtre de Vidy-Lausanne in 2004 in its French version, *Essaim*, translated by Judith Revel. It was then restaged at the Théâtre National de la Colline in Paris in 2005, with Évelyne Didi, Gabriel Scotti (original music), Alexandre Simon (video), Jacques Gebel (paintings), and Claire Sternberg (set design), in a production directed by Barbara Nicolier. In June 2005, the play was also performed by the students of the theater workshop of the Université de Paris I Panthéon-Sorbonne at the Théâtre National de la Colline, directed by Barbara Nicolier. In 2006, the Italian version, *Sciame*, was staged by Sandro Mabellini in Rome. In January 2009, the German version, *Schwarm*, was staged by Christina Schlüter at the Theater Bielefeld in a translation by Gerda Poschmann.

In 2006, *The Bent Man* was staged in the original Italian version, *L'uomo piegato*, in Rome and Viterbo in a production directed by Pierpaolo Sepe, then restaged in 2007 at the Burgtheater in Vienna.

Cithaeron was performed by the students of the theater workshop of the Université de Paris I Panthéon-Sorbonne at the Théâtre National de la Colline in June 2007 in a production directed by Barbara Nicolier.

All three plays in *Trilogy of Resistance* were given a public reading on October 14, 2007, at the Théâtre National de la Colline by Gilles David, Évelyne Didi, and Pierre-Félix Gravière and with the participation of Judith Revel, Antonio Negri, Alain Françon, Ruth Olaizola, Jean-François Peyret, and the youngest members of the Radio France music school. In February 2008, this reading was broadcast by France Culture under the auspices of the series *Fictions et cie,* a production of Jean Couturier in collaboration with Barbara Nicolier. A performance of the complete *Trilogy* by the students of the theater workshop of the Sorbonne, directed by Barbara Nicolier, was given June 26–27, 2009, at the Théâtre National de la Colline.

SWARM

DIDACTICS OF THE MILITANT
2004

SWARM: DIDACTICS OF THE MILITANT

MAN
CHORUS

Scene AI. Indignation[1]

MAN *(waking with difficulty)*: Indignation fills my poor life. This morning, when I woke up, I once again had trouble breathing. I felt the weight of those who are suffering, I felt the absurd movement of it. An unrestrained movement, a weight that sickens. An unbearable sensation.

The man who gathers up his miserable rags after an icy night passed outdoors. The comrade, graying under the harness, who leaves prison each morning and whom the harshness of imprisonment has not yet succeeded in bending. The unemployed in search of a wage. The illegal immigrant butchered by work for a pittance. The sick one sent suffering to the hospital. The addict who ends up destroyed by his last fix. In short, all the poor, all the desperate . . .

He reads the newspaper.

This one who was the victim of assassination, that one who was the victim of the law, this one who is enduring apartheid and that one who seeks to escape it and gets shipwrecked, this one who is massacred by precision bombing and that one who falls under its collateral effects, this one with an empty stomach and that one who thirsts for justice . . . They are all here in front of me, the rich and the poor: I don't know what outrages me the most—private wealth that always grows ever larger or the common poverty that extends over increasingly vast spaces. They say that a new society will soon be born out of the shell of the old. What's certain is the fact that the old society is dead, but between the society that no longer exists and the one whose coming is proclaimed, the only link is pain and tears.[2]

He reflects.

Solitude: is that the novelty, the *quidditas* of the society that is still to come? I don't think so. What I myself believe is that this novelty creates the conditions for an extreme alienation, a ferocious form of inequality and separation.

CHORUS: Didn't they promise that this new society would expand freedom, progress, and intelligence?

Didn't they say that intelligence would become common and that it would produce equality?

But solitude destroys all the desires of common practices and lives, solidarity and cooperation become the abstract images of a road that is impossible to follow. The words of all those who have regaled us with these sweet dreams, those very words are transformed little by little into mad and destructive stammers. But where is that famous human brain, capable of the greatest undertakings and the most radical liberation, where is that community of labor and spirit that modernity promised us?

MAN (*responding to* **CHORUS**): Perhaps the only way that remains for us to rediscover this hope is to seek it through a computer screen . . . No, that too is a history of solitude, what's the point of it? What we lack is the very desire for novelty, creation, invention.

Compassion for this tired world that surrounds me is a sadness born from the evils that I see too many beloved persons endure. Indignation shatters the singular continuity of desire, sends it back to us in pieces, often aimed at something else or simply neutralized. But isn't this the true frontier of despair? This morning, every morning, my life is obsessed with indignation, its potent reality and its insurmountable effects.

CHORUS: Indignation—the only light that suddenly crosses obscurity, the only heat that warms during the days of winter: a God who appears not in order to exhibit his existence but in order to illuminate your despair.

MAN: I am blinded by it.

In this scene, the **CHORUS** *has followed and reinforced the* **MAN**'s *doubt and indignation.*

Scene A2. Hatred

CHORUS: You are a prisoner of impotence, of despair, you are mired in the lead of defeat . . . But didn't you build this prison of yours with your own hands?

MAN: No, the indignation I feel is the only form of resistance I have managed to develop! The other day, I made a young girl cry because I reacted sarcastically to her emotion: she had just discovered injustice. That's how it goes in the world, I told her, with all the scorn I was capable of when faced with her soul in revolt . . .

CHORUS: The indignation you feel is resistance that is turning negative. You will end up tearing out your heart like the birds of ill omen do. You won't feel compassion, just hatred. A blind passion that turns back against the one who clasps your throat in a slipknot . . .

MAN: The advantage of hatred is that it allows you to recognize and identify suffering for what it is: the product of an adversary. There is an enemy, a very potent enemy, who is suffocating us; a master of exploitation who exercises his dominion over men, a ferocious God! It's an atrocious, transcendent asymmetry, a power that totally invests the depth of life, that occupies it, sucking out the very substance, emptying out the potency! I feel the arrogance of the enemy, I am subjected to it, I endure it . . . An implacable suffering that indignation never succeeds in calming. I need to act, I need to strike, I need to avenge!

CHORUS: Hatred is a passion that is just as active as love, but it doesn't construct anything, it is limited to destroying for destruction's sake, unfailingly. So, try it! Act!

MAN: Hatred leaves me alone . . . No, not totally alone: we are at least two, because there is always the one who exploits me and dominates me, the one who takes his bread from my brother, the one who steals his imagination from the dreamer . . . him, and me. I want to make my hatred into a weapon, an act.

CHORUS: But this will of yours, doesn't it exhaust itself in the disproportion you are facing? The enemy is stronger, the measure of his violence is extreme. If your hatred provokes the enemy, isn't that because it resembles him even before it has managed to express itself, and thus it provokes in advance a still more violent reaction?

MAN: Of course, the enemy's power is infinitely greater than what my hatred can express, and he responds to my demand for justice with the unequal violence of war . . . but if war ceases to be something abstract, if it is not merely a nightmare, then it becomes the arrogance of the master who day after day unleashes it against each one of us, against our hatred, but also against our love. Here my spirit's hesitation becomes a decision for vengeance, a wish to strike. I must break this tension that overcomes me, I want this pig to die. I'm becoming delirious, and yet I continue to feel my body torn apart by the desire for violence. Whatever you want, it couldn't be worse. Will hatred for this enemy who constrains us to war become thus the sun of our lives? Our life unfolds under the permanent threat of an imposed war, within the everyday sorrows of exploitation and alienation . . .

(He shakes himself and begins to stir.)

I wake up and I go to work. But there is no work . . . and when there is work, it's short-lived, precarious, miserable work. At each instant of existence, it seems that one must choose between life and death. The freedom of work—that could be the adventure of being, but it has become the power of the master.

(*He addresses the* **CHORUS**.)

But you, don't you feel it, this hatred that overcomes the flesh, that undermines the will, that dominates our destiny? Not only mine, but that of this poor generation that has been deprived of every hope for the future.

CHORUS: No, you are alone. Don't imagine you are the expression of a world, a generation . . . You are alone . . . You and him, the slave and the master. There is no philosophy of redemption that would be capable of helping you absorb this sorrow, this humiliation. There is no consolation. If you clap your hands, if you scream, you will hear no echo. The valley in which you live is deaf. So, try it, act! Perhaps awakening the consciousness of a single person is enough to allow all the others to rediscover the desire for rebellion. The fall of a single drop of water can create a river that will make the valley resound once again.

The **CHORUS** *has revived the* **MAN** *and driven him to action.*

Scene A3. Temptation

MAN: Hatred of the enemy, this absolute hatred that nourishes me, in this resides my only hope.

The temptation of the martyr, the ultimate and total sacrifice, the reversal of the asymmetry of power, its nullification through extreme resistance, to the point of suicide, if necessary . . . My body against their power! The great wind of human vengeance!

CHORUS: The bare potency of the body exposes itself, as strong and violent as the enormous and irresistible machine of power. The tyranny of power confronts resistance . . .

But is this true? When you tell us this, we feel the emotion of this great scandal that is the affirmation of a bare life . . . But how can all this give a name to resistance?

MAN: Resistance: my indignation, my hatred . . . This is how the scandal becomes a hurricane and bare life is redeemed by a burst of rebellion.

CHORUS: Thus the suicide bomber is the justified response of the naked man faced with power's will to destruction?

MAN: He kills himself, this man alone, because he wants to destroy the greatest possible number of the objects of his hatred—those with which the persecutor tortures him. And these objects are men, other men, who are obliged to be pawns in the hands of power . . . It's my indignation that kills them. Because I am a man alone.

CHORUS: Temptation is a geometrical potency. Religions have demonstrated geometrically the capacity of sacrifice to reduce the infinite difference between man and God to a possible equation. It is in this way that Christ is truly human. The rebel nature of divine invention appears here: vengeance is also redemption, *nemesis* is also a *catharsis*.

MAN: So, what must I do? You live within the contradiction. You tell me to act, but you ceaselessly insist on my solitude. Do you, you too, want to be my adversary? What must I do?

You have not cleared it up for me. My friends, my comrades, you endure the same solitude as mine. Despair bends your knees, misery numbs the nerves of your brains. Your nakedness: you cover it like men and women who have sinned. But our misery does not deserve the sorrow of silence and shame, our nakedness is proud.

I must do it. There, I put on my clothing, I cover my nakedness with explosives.

(He slowly begins to dress himself by covering his body with explosives before donning his clothing.)

A bomb in the front pocket, some explosives in a backpack, a heavily loaded belt, the detonator in the pocket most quickly at hand . . . or else simply a gun: to shoot all those who do me wrong, those whose every move I know, day or night, whenever I want. They call me terrorist, suicide bomber, assassin. So, what. To die, yes, but dreaming of the groans of a massacred enemy, the terrified screams of those I will have wounded and mutilated . . . thus.

CHORUS: Martyr or hero? Heroism is secular martyrdom, just as the martyr is a religious hero: the gesture of immanence can be translated into the religious temptation just as the secular gesture can be lived as transcendence . . .

MAN: My monk's habit of explosives is ready, I hold my arsenal close under my belt.

CHORUS: Your hatred appears like a robe of justice. They have pushed you to this.

MAN: The monstrous force of power arrayed before me leaves me no choice.

CHORUS: It is a reasonable ideology to want to re-create a certain symmetry, the normality of a life that would no longer merely be marked by the wound of injustice . . .

MAN: Here is my death, my death in order to kill.

CHORUS: Thus, only your indignation manages to speak and elude the impotent stammering of those who let themselves be persuaded, the fearful chatter only slaves use. Thus, only your hatred can be transformed into action, and its violence seeks to re-create something like freedom, to become love once again.

MAN: My act is necessary. When I move across this terrain, everything at once comes to life around me. The baroque emptiness of the world of power, this black colony of terror appears brutally in broad daylight. They call me a terrorist. But what I'm plunging into right now, isn't it the water of life?

The **CHORUS** *began by arguing with the* **MAN**, *then it responds to his rationale.*

Scene BI. In Profundo Gurgite

Loud sounds coming from a distance . . . HERE RUPTURE, THE
HEIGHT OF NEGATIVITY . . .

MAN: No! I'm suffocating, drowning in that sea! Everything is spent
and lost in this war, everything looks like death and destruction,
everything ends up becoming equivalent to everything else . . . The
dynamite I'm carrying wrapped around me has a weight that
engulfs me . . . I no longer manage it, I no longer bear the decision I
made . . . Was this truly a decision? Or simply the response to a provocation from power? The search for something as potent as power?
Am I not enchanted by these peculiar sirens? Instead of annihilating
force, was I not on the contrary in the process of reproducing it?

CHORUS: Dying to kill: are you really sure about what you're doing?
This doesn't touch the potency of indignation, it merely exacerbates
the solitude of hatred. Are you sure that nakedness is not composed
of other weights? Are you sure your naked body is really light? Filled
with dynamite, you go straight down. Even the lightest piece of cork
can't remain on the surface if it is weighed down with the corruption
of this world's waters. Even children drown—innocence suffocates;
birds don't fly in the void. Dying for justice: the stammering of madness, killing for justice and becoming a monster of power. Is it true or
false? How can we act in this deep sea? By repeating the miracle of
the fish that transformed itself into a bird, and by inventing the metamorphosis of hatred into love? Force is perhaps not the only resource
of resistance.

MAN: There has to be something else in resistance, because I see it as
sweet, singular, irresistible . . . An act of love. Often I think it is only
when my resistance is rising that I have truly loved; that's when my
flesh is alive and my body is engaged . . . No, the will to kill and the
drive toward death cannot be gestures of desire . . . But I must face
force, this enormous thing that is power: only an absolute act can
face it . . .

CHORUS: Calm down. Things are not as absolute as you believe. What you say is true: all around us nature seems to have gone mad, like in bad horror films: a landscape of war, the landscape of the arrogance of power, the violence of the imperial appropriation of life and the wealth of others, the external grip on existence and the construction of nations . . . Tanks, long lines of militia with weapons, radar, networks of coded messages, superpower, strategic strikes accompanied by endless collateral effects . . . Obviously, this is horrible . . . But look there, my friend, look at what's happening behind you . . . yes, back there, in the corner, there are shadows appearing and immediately vanishing . . . Is resistance organizing? Perhaps, perhaps, they are so numerous . . . These shadows are the expressions of a common reality, an immense force . . . You cannot act all alone, throw down your arms!

MAN: No, don't try to fool me! I have always wanted to visit the giants, who were compelled to exceed the measure of the gods' commandment by an accident of nature, an unforeseen event . . . Don't tell me this freedom is coming! I don't see it. Don't tell me the rain of atoms is interrupted by the freedom of the *clinamen,* that some Iphigenia is raising the winds of revolution! I don't see it. Am I blind? I am here, both armored and stripped naked by the desire to kill . . .

CHORUS: Disoriented by a confrontation over the meaning of being and love, indignation, and hatred . . . War machines traverse your soul. They all come back to the same thing.

MAN: My mouth is dry, I no longer know where I am, I am agitated. *In profundis gurgite:* everything that my body bears, these weapons give it a new form and deceive the flesh of the man I am—this desire makes me exist.

*The **CHORUS** has ironized pedagogically on the **MAN**'s tragedy.*

Scene B2. Disenchantment (ENTZAUBERUNG)

MAN: I no longer know how to escape from doubt and disorienta-tion. The more I load my body with explosives, the more I clean my weapons, the heavier I become; but this heaviness of the body is not life. Life is an event of the flesh . . . Why must I reduce my body to dead flesh in order to make life possible? Why? I am lost, I don't know how to answer. This is the flesh that I have in common with other men—all those who suffer and rebel—this is the flesh that I am in the process of sacrificing.

CHORUS: You really believe it is possible to annihilate the flesh? Don't fool yourself, the flesh is not an abstract substance, it's more than your own body, more than your own spirit, more than simple matter, it's a principle that gives form to life and offers it a singular rhythm—at the point where, before, there was only quantity and movement. Flesh is like water, earth, fire, and air: one of the primordial and irre-ducible elements by means of which being is given, as the Ancients said . . . Across the body of each of us, flesh invents the singularity of life. Flesh is the common of multiplicity.

MAN: Rather than thinking of the death that kills, must I thus plunge my desire into this common of the flesh? A common that my will to die destroys even as it seeks to renew it?

CHORUS: The common is the passion that grows and develops in the life of each of us. The common is the passage from "I" to "we"—the condition and result of life together. It is the language that is seized from the Other, living labor, the body that rediscovers its flesh in production and in cooperation.

MAN (*suddenly seized by passion*): How can the enchantment of the common that you are proposing to me be a disenchantment of indignation and despair? How can it tear me away from my desire to kill? Oh! How I would like to be able to recognize that my flesh is the same as that of the giants who appeared at the same time as the revolution of *homo novus*! Figures of freedom, that's what we need: we want new giants who could put the flesh to work in freedom and innovation . . . But I, ready to die in order to kill, what must I do now? My task is monstrous, just as my body laden with explosives and my armed hand have suddenly become . . . Isn't an explosion of life still possible, despite everything?

He begins to undress slowly, hesitantly at the start and then more and more hurriedly.

CHORUS: God, if only you existed! If you really sent angels to guide our spirits, you would show us how to react to the enemy through creation and not by destroying: by exalting the flesh that creates the common of life! But the God of Hosts disdains this mission and protects the suicide bombers with his benediction. Bastard transcendence, haven't you made enough people suffer? Curse you, don't you know how painful it is to confine the force of giants within the cage of monsters?

MAN: Calmly, slowly, softly, do not hurry, the explosives are fragile, the weapon is dangerous, try to remove everything.

The **CHORUS** *has accompanied the* **MAN** *in his choices.*

Scene B3. Kairòs

More light: no longer an enclosed space but the entrance to a square.

CHORUS: *Kairòs:* the instant when the arrow flies from the bow. Doubt cannot last. Coming to an end does not mean being isolated: the ivory tower is shattered—that of the sovereign Ego, that of liberation, that of counterpower. Only resistance remains. But resistance is enough: to the Ego it opposes the we, to liberation freedom, to counterpower the invention of another life. Resistance is the daughter of love and poverty, a poverty that was prepared for death but that has been awakened by love. *Kairòs* is sudden and yet continuous, like the stammering of a child searching for words to speak, to say. *Kairòs* goes beyond poverty, *kairòs* acts out love. Here the will to live is revealed, the potency of the flesh becomes mistress of life. Here indignation and hatred stop submitting to vengeance and discover with joy and something like elation a shadow of justice.

MAN *(He continues to remove the explosives with which he was armored.)*: Words are never effective enough to reconstruct the tension that exists in the passage from meaning to action. I looked death in the eye because I was blind. I looked death in the eye, and at that very moment I saw into myself, through my own eyes, I had succeeded in turning my gaze upon the flesh—or is it God that I saw?

It may be that this light I am about to enter is blinding, that this place where I seek to go refuses me and despises me. Be careful, calm down, act slowly, don't hurry, the others are fragile, the world can be dangerous. Try to remove everything. No, don't be afraid: there is something new under the sun.

CHORUS: *Kairòs* is there, like a dancing child—a difficult dance that risks itself on the edge of the void of being, that rushes into the unrecognized region of novelty, and yet it remains a child's dance . . . A joy that needs no prudence in order to offer itself to sight . . .

MAN: I touch my body, I look at others, I have anew the experience of meaning just when I thought that orgasm had been annihilated by confusion, and that the tyrannical power of the enemy had neutralized the generative capacity that was mine—when the others, all the others, were not bodies but shadows of power. No, this corruption that was imposed on me by force, despite everything I manage to avoid it. And I tear the veil away from the mystery of power. Power lives off of my obedience.

CHORUS: The necessity of power is only the fetish of an impotence and a poverty that don't know how to revolt.

MAN: Here is the moment in which I rediscover my strength, I embrace it like a loved one desired for a long time in my dreams.

CHORUS: The settling of time's scores is quickening, the days are filling up: it's useless to descend into hell or to climb Calvary in order to rebel. All we need is to let the flesh love and transform desire into action. At each moment. It's life, not a dark fable in which man is his own enemy . . . Life is a moment of creation followed by yet another moment of creation, always, without end, because man is a multitude of these creative moments that are interconnected by a language of love.

MAN: When I rediscover the desire of life, I rediscover it in the form of the multitude.

My poor life, I caress you, and in each spot of flesh that I touch, a world of passion reveals itself. Everything on which my eye falls is a whirlpool of images that grabs me. But passion is an action: don't you see it, from far away, this light of the multitude in motion?

CHORUS: Common action, common being, constituent immediacy . . .

MAN: If my resistance doesn't want to produce death, it must construct life, it must constitute itself in collective life. To resist is to return to oneself, because above all it is to place your own life in the midst of the life of all the others, to construct life together, piece by piece . . . To resist.

CHORUS: To resist is to decide that life is worth more than death. When you refuse the destructive force of the link that ties life and death together, resistance can be taken completely into being, without any possible outside.

MAN: My resistance is absolute freedom. It does not arise from horizons of value that range beyond what freedom is possible, it negates all the processes of liberation because it is already free and it knows it, and this is what makes it strong. My martyrdom, I want to come back to it like an old sock and transform it into a direct testimony of freedom. Of course, death can still strike me at any moment, but my testimony will never again be lived ascetically, nor will it give birth to a mystical ontology. Asceticism, mysticism are moralities that today are found inside the viscera of power. Rebellion is quite different: it is imagination and joy.

The **CHORUS** *has led the* **MAN** *on his way.*

Scene CI. Resistance

MAN *(finally setting down the last explosive charge)*: Now that I have set down the last explosive charge, my nakedness is exposed to the gaze of others. I am ashamed. I want to cover this nakedness that is now my own. How can I dress it again in the affects and warmth of friends, in intellectual complicities and exchanges? How can I put it at the disposal of a project of love?

CHORUS *(sarcastically)*: Stop, you are filling your life with senseless rhetoric of the brain, language, and paradoxes! Have you gone mad? Perhaps you believe that the enemy's strength is so weak at this point that your words can now vanquish it? Are you claiming that love can construct a life that knows nothing of death? Have you gone mad? Give us an example of your sublime freedom! Saint Francis too was vanquished—and his own brothers jammed the sharpened tip of power into his heart. Idealism and utopia are not foods that can be digested by the starving stomach of the poor.

MAN: I can't go on like this! I must make a decision, I must make a choice. And I know that it's not like my decision could act as a North Star in the tragedy of the real. It's true, I'm mad, we're all mad. But now that I am naked, I rediscover myself and I discover that I am perhaps multiple—there, now I can decide because I have recognized the others.

CHORUS: Your nakedness is thus the paradoxical discovery of a common life. Look: he re-covers his body with the clothes of others, men and women, young and old, white and black! Here comes the potent harlequin!

MAN: I ask myself what only the multitude can answer. I want to become multitude, and I know that only nakedness can make me discover it. No, I don't ask it of myself alone, but of you too, my friends, my comrades: you too, you can experience nakedness as the solitary condition of the rebellion of the many. Poor and excluded ones, imprisoned and stupefied in the framework of power . . . and yet: within this very framework, having become a multitude despite everything, let's help each other to renew the desire of the flesh and demonstrate the strength of our transformation on the basis of our nakedness.

CHORUS: We have succeeded in being naked, poor, and incapable of naming things. We have succeeded in emptying out and recomposing the too-well-known names of rebellion and insurrection through the experience of poverty. In this dialogue that ties us to you, we feel the common emerging like a creative apparatus.

MAN: I've known them for a very long time, these names and these passions. By stripping myself naked, I've reached the source of life: by means of poverty I have touched the lowest point of existence; but that point is not one of solitude because poverty is common. Through poverty I am a multitude. You're right, we've gone mad.

CHORUS: Resistance constructs worlds of madness . . .

MAN: Bizarre lunatics that the psych ward excites and separates: sublime witnesses of reality, embracing truth, capable of opening poverty to desire and teaching desire to act.

CHORUS: The resister constructs a new world from below. By his mere existence he threatens the cynicism of the bourgeoisie, monetary alienation, the expropriation of life, the exploitation of labor, the colonization of the affects. Here indignation finds its new insurrection.

The resister's poverty is his wealth. Take up your body once again! Discover the common life, make generosity into a hammer for driving the nail of virtue into truth.

The **CHORUS**'s *behavior has oscillated between sarcasm and benevolence.*

Scene C2. Ideology

CHORUS: *"I am the Angel of Despair. With my hands I dispense ecstasy, numbness, oblivion, the lust and torment of the body. My language is silence, my song the scream. Terror dwells in the shadows of my wings. My hope is the last gasp. My hope is the first battle. I am the knife with which the dead pry open the coffin. I am the one who will be. My flight is the rebellion, my heaven the abyss of tomorrow."*[3]

MAN: Ah, what an unlucky angel!

CHORUS: They told us that behind the back of the *angelus novus* we could find only a landscape of ruins, destruction, and misery; and that only on the basis of catastrophe could hope finally rise again.[4] This is just ideology.

MAN: Now I join to my pain a fury toward everything that led me to this despair. Yes, the desire to live the new can be born on the basis of the nakedness that I experienced. But for this to come about, I must destroy the calcified memory of tradition . . . The classical texts? Exactly! They are now the rags of betrayal. I tear them to pieces: with these plucked pages I could cover my shame. They no longer nourish my militant decision, because my decision is now different: it's a fury of clarity, a hatred of betrayal, a passion for common action.

CHORUS: Ideology is a toad that spits venom: if it strikes your eyes, you will go blind. A legend, yes, for the toad, but not for ideology. Ideology: a transmitted knowledge, a vanguard knowledge, a knowledge only for the few, that claims to contain everything in itself and to bring the passion of the great many to fruition in its totality. Sometimes ideology seems to function, but this is an illusion: the train that departs is not yours, it's the one next to it. Even when ideology wins it is false, because it absorbs the truth into power. Everything that happens is reduced to it. And when the experience of struggles maddens it, then ideology describes these same struggles as a set of errors and catastrophes. Idealism and the vanguard that are confused in ideology cannot bear suffering and consider struggles to be a source of pain. What hypocrisy!

MAN: But I see something quite different in the past: multitudes who struggle ceaselessly—massive, aleatory, singular. Each of their defeats, despite everything, has always been a victory: a way of pushing back fear, a refusal of fate, an event, a singular decision.

CHORUS: Beyond every ideology, beyond the vanguards, in resistance, the poor and the exploited are multitudes in motion. Resistance and rebellion are the most widely shared decisions in the world. They are nourished on the desire for life, not the putridity of death. The dialogue with the past can and does recognize what is living.

MAN: For me too: every desire I feel recognizes a cell that produced it in the past. Now that I know myself to be the product of the multitude, I can no longer accept the solitary halo of the combatant, the contracted decision of vanguard consciousnesses, the totality that it professes: they don't open up hope, they crush it. But we are not armed Jesuits, we have no need of spiritual exercises in order to resist. The only possible vanguard is the multitude.

CHORUS: They assert as well that the grass must be cut down so that it will grow back more vigorously, and desire must adapt to necessity so that it will blossom. There you have the syllogisms of an obstinate will that continually fails to distinguish between the frustration of need and the realization of dreamy desires . . .

MAN: No! The flux of history is like the sea's undertow, it always returns like the seasons—and there are no storms or shipwrecks, no maritime glory or happy springtime that could efface this potency. When it has been nourished by the manure of death, grass doesn't grow back. Only life nourishes life. Killing an enemy doesn't make the meadows greener. Dying a hero doesn't make desire more real. Only by stepping back from necessity does one make freedom effective. Why, then, despite everything, am I always petrified by the incessant call of ideology? The medusa fascinates me. No, it's a phantom that torments me, a specter that haunts me, a corporal or a priest who still claims to give me orders . . .

CHORUS: Faith, still faith, for these men who would like to be free to create a world, happy with a possibility that is offered them . . . Ideology only proposes a block, a sticky totality to which only the faithful can have access . . . But in the face of this fluid and stifling mass of ideology, each refusal ends up succumbing to its inert violence: thus the space of the possible is sterilized . . . Ideology is the religion of necessity, even when it takes the form of an ideology of freedom. Only life can give us life. And this is because at its origin life is action: action is the only grass that always grows back. When it leads to hatred, indignation is not action. Ideological drift slides over the totality without undermining it, and that's how martyrdom ripens . . .

MAN: When indignation opens itself up to love and thought rediscovers action, then the poor man I am feels himself freed from this miserable transcendence that paralyzed him . . . I know myself to be active, ready, tuned in, like a Mother Courage seeking food for her children.

CHORUS: You are just barely beginning to understand this reality that is called immanence. A world that is henceforth flat, smooth, and indefinite opens up before you. That world is aleatory, it offers you a thousand flight paths and a thousand courses of action . . .

MAN: My mother, who lived on an immense plain along a large river, told me repeatedly that the passions are always transparent and strong. The plane of immanence accepts no obstacle that could block the view. My strength is invisible because it overcomes every obstacle. That's how my passion begins to grow, a passion that discovers that it can project itself onto the world, that it can always become more consistent, that it can be revived endlessly by the diagram of desire . . .

I find myself, ultimately, with the others: not in the illusion and the lie of ideology, but in the joy of a common action.

The **CHORUS** *has clarified the* **MAN**'s *thoughts.*

Scene C3. Party

CHORUS: From now on we are old. Recall the discussion we had: it's not a matter of a medusa, it's our own history, we've been the voice of all that. Remember the party . . .

(The **CHORUS** *is transformed into a parody of a Red Army chorus, the men singing while stiffly saluting.)*

Nothing is possible when one is alone, only the party can make us effective, all together we advance holding hands. The party multiplies militancy, it transforms us into a compact little group, we advance holding hands. Each in his place, we communicate our revolution-ary know-how and passion, we advance holding hands . . . We are the spark that starts a prairie fire,[5] only our union will save the life of those who fall into the fire, we advance holding hands . . .

MAN *(Captivated by the illusion, he joins the singers, strikes the pose, and sings in his turn.)*: Victory lies not in a singularity become multitude and ultimately incarnating the dignity of the revolution. No, let us ask the totality, let us ask the class, let us ask the vanguards, because they are the ones who make history and who win . . . The singularity is a martyr who opposes the power of the class's enemy and nothing else, nothing else . . .

The **CHORUS** *no longer sings, it mouths maxims.*

CHORUS: When you belong to the corps of revolutionaries, you must be ready to die and kill for the revolution! The norm, the decision, the measure belong to the party . . .

A dissonant sound, sharp and very loud, brutally interrupts the **CHORUS**.

MAN: No! No! The thought of death is becoming stronger again: not through ideological doubt and fog but in lived experience! But I know it, death—and the power of its illusion! I know how strong it has been, I know how it marks our bodies, their history, their imaginary . . .

(He dreams, eyes open.)

My grandfather . . . there he is: a worker who leads his companions in revolt, with those who fell during the great strikes, in the struggles against the war, in the confrontations with the police . . . His father still used a cart, and during the long nights of the month of August, while the slow steps of the oxen gave him the rhythm, he loaded it up with the poor children of the other laborers in order to teach them the names of the stars . . . Today, we have forgotten the names of the stars. We speak of unity among the classes. The price of liberation is death . . .

My father . . . that's another story, things change . . . A communist too, but another history begins. Of course, they still die—the whole history of my communist family is a litany of the dead. Existence has become a mortifying expanse: the deserter, the antifascist bandit, the partisan, my father . . . The light of sacrifice is no longer only what the party demands, it has become the expression of a desire for freedom that struggle incarnates . . . The discipline of the totality dissolves into the adherence to a cause in which freedom itself is its own light.

CHORUS: More of the mystical body, just triumphant flesh . . . Communism is not out there, in the promise of a radiant future, but here and now: it's a construction that proclaims itself.

MAN *(dreaming once again)*: There you have it, the new generation of those who don't believe that communism is a utopia placed before them, but on the contrary a desire for themselves at its most profound. An event is produced on the ruins of ideology, against every utopia: I've seen millions of my brothers fight against the war. Singularity no longer has any need of totality, it rises up against death. Here and there, and then elsewhere, always more, appearing and disappearing like a flock of migrating birds crossing the sky in strange and ever new forms, coming together and splitting apart according to the spirit of the trip and the hope . . .

MAN and **CHORUS** *(together)*: All together, we are potency, we no longer want to hear talk of power. The martyr no longer represents humanity. We have launched a life machine—and even if death is once again thrust forward by the arms of power, like it was at Genoa, even if the beast bit into the helpless joy of youth, the multitude is there: in order to oppose it.

The **MAN** *and the* **CHORUS** *reunite on the basis of the critique of the party.*

Scene DI. Swarm

CHORUS *(All the voices forming the* **CHORUS** *are now totally different from one another.)*: —Thus is revealed the militancy of singularities. Resistance is a diffuse force that gathers itself up and attacks from one side or the other, that invents its own networks and expresses aggressiveness through them—thousands and thousands of actions that disorient the adversary, a live swarming that takes unexpected forms and irresistible dimensions . . .

— Let's go, friends! To the barricades!

— Flexible, precarious, mobile workers, make your weakness into strength, invent a new May Day of joy and mass intellectuality, a "rave" that crosses metropolises!

— Let's go, friends! To the barricades!

— Let's go, multitude of freedom!

— Surround capital in all the workplaces!

— Sabotage, disorder, militancy! Add viruses to the blackouts, senseless drifting to potent projects of knowledge, introduce the biopolitics of insurrection into the language of science!

— But above all: reappropriate the maximum of productive force! Take back everything! Load your brain like a rifle and free your imagination, invent new worlds!

— Capital lusts after the vital alternative that you represent, and fears it. Its power aims to retake control.

— Living in a swarm goes far beyond the simple threshold of disciplinary order. A century of struggles has destroyed the possibility of disciplines. Fighting and attacking in a swarm inspires paranoia in the enemy. Don't let him reflect.

— How could he answer you?

— By privatizing existence, by feudalizing it, by bantustaning it.

By raising walls of separation, by producing new imperial dependencies . . . Nevertheless, this repetitive and inert defense has never really worked: capital is henceforth a parasite, it no longer possesses the rationale of development.

— The truncheon of command remains, but it is a bent truncheon. It can impose its will only when the swarm is thinned out and the horizon seems to become visible again.

—But suddenly, the productive force of workers, intellectuals, peasants, women, immigrants, and all the poor resumes: for the boss, the fog lifts once again; for power, an opaque and impractical rain resumes, a lightless tempest; for capital, a living barrier rears up: a different production, of singularities that nothing stops . . .

— Not a simple obstacle, a limit . . . A limit as high as an insurmountable mountain can be, as deep as a vertiginous chasm can be . . .

— Chasm! *In profundo gurgite*! There where our resistance was broken, where our indignation was dissolved . . .

MAN: I have lived the plunge into life, into its precipitate transformation, as a moment of disorientation . . . We continue to seek the One, the Party, Ideology . . . But I know now that I have found myself and I have found others, others to infinity, the common of the multitude. Swarm.

(He turns his back to the audience and reflects.)

What we have found is a "we"—a collective, of course, but made of singularities; a set of actions, desires, decisions. If there is something like a collective today, this is because it constructs itself by looking within itself—no transcendental, no master, they simply rely on a father or a mother who can organize or explain it: the collective gaze into itself is the common of the swarm. No origin, no principle—but a proliferation, a coming and going, an arabesque that develops the order of singularities into ever more radical and contiguous forms of being-together. Swarm. An ordered form that is impossible to contain, the form of collective singularity and subjectivity. Swarm.

Scene D2. Metamorphosis

CHORUS: This is how the metamorphosis of the subject is produced. Up to now, there was a way of working and struggling that hung from the chain of the big factory: and the masses, their strength indifferent to singularity, constituted the body of the revolutionary movement. Today, each singularity puts the multitude of affects, capacities, and passions that constitute it to work. This is how the social labor of the swarm-worker is born. Man, speak to us, tell us what the discovery of the "we" of the swarm means!

MAN: I feel totally new. With you I have freely constructed a common desire and a project of action. We: we are as common as the layers of this earth that the rains and winds have accumulated—different and yet inseparable from now on. It is difficult, this metamorphosis: we taste the desert sand that the sirocco has left in our mouths. Yesterday and throughout the centuries.

CHORUS: The resistance of the swarm is revealed through the network that it establishes, its ways of diffusing and concentrating itself are instantaneous—it's a cloud in the form of a sword. But who is there to wield the sword? Who decides?

MAN: It was easy to choose the moment of attack when the vanguards knew the future and the Party had stored up weapons! No, pardon comrades, it was not so easy as that . . . but it had meaning, and the occasion could be favorable . . . It was not easy because criticism and self-criticism tortured us, insurrection was always at the center of the debate . . . And now? The swarm seems on the contrary to live in immediacy, and its motion is never suspended by the long fatigue of reflection, on the contrary . . .

CHORUS: On the contrary . . . For something is produced in there, as if the symptom was revealed in the result, because the decision to attack traversed the entire swarm intensely—traversed the other way: each singularity that constitutes the multitude is in turn a multitude, and this is how one's indignation gets mixed up with the other's, and this is how love, generosity, the will to struggle, and the passion for new being become possible . . .

MAN: So this is my decision: it is born of this metamorphosed body, of this agile giant made of a new potency. The decision, for me, is when the multitude begins to produce. I feel the decision like an unexpected leap of being, like a rupture in the repetition of the past, like an unforeseen and yet hoped-for future. The decision is the event, this metamorphosis not only of nature but of time.

CHORUS: The decision is the condensation of an immense constellation into the sun, it's the explosion of a nebula of atoms, it's the *clinamen* of life. It's by way of the decision that the metamorphosis of life exists and the revolution is possible.

The **MAN** *and the* **CHORUS** *lead the discussion together from here on.*

Scene D3. Exodus

CHORUS: We live the event, we are the swarm, we produce the metamorphosis: that's what is called exodus. This is how we abandon power: what we want is a different life. We go toward it by attacking, because power cannot live without sucking our blood and it now seeks to imprison us.

MAN: Pharaoh's army pursues us. We go away after having cruelly inflicted on Egypt the plagues that only the indignation of a real God could invent: we are innocent of God's cruelty. Aaron's rear guard defends the swarm's flight toward the sea—a sea that is green like our hope, red like the blood of Egypt's defeat. Beyond the sea the desert awaits us, the long march, experimentation with our potency. Life and death continue to give rhythm to our existence, just as the dawn and the dusk allow the day to take shape: but life is free, henceforth, and the day is potency, and the night is love.

CHORUS: Power cannot produce or reproduce itself without exploiting: exploitation consists in sinking teeth into the life, freedom, and creativity of man, shredding them, digesting them. The flesh of man is the primary material of exploitation, the body of power. Freedom lies only in going away, in choosing exodus. Going away: far from this horrible slaughterhouse that is life when it is bent under the sovereign power of capital.

MAN: Defend us, Aaron, prevent the beast from crushing us until the impossible is ultimately produced and the sea finally parts . . .

CHORUS: The impossible has taken place. Exodus has become possible. Utopia is henceforth behind us. Our success, the opening of the impossible, the verification of virtue!

MAN: Only love resembles exodus because love is not the son of poverty and wealth but is itself Diotima, the risk of a potency that does not hesitate to throw itself into the void of being, onto the edge of the future.

CHORUS: Love and exodus do not travel, they generate. That is virtue.

MAN: Under the tents of the multitude in exodus, we feel joy. The night, the desert land trembles with amorous throbbing and the sky is filled with luminous messages. Stellar fraternities . . . Children construct beautiful statues of sand; every time the desert softens, the adults construct the outposts of a possible city.

But even if the path is long, we will never tire of traveling it. After having experienced the desire for death so acutely, and the necessity to kill with so much pain, we know henceforth—I know henceforth—that a new world is possible, a world of the living, a world of lovers.

THE BENT MAN |

DIDACTICS OF THE REBEL
2005

THE BENT MAN: DIDACTICS OF THE REBEL

CHORUS
FRIEND
MAN
WIFE
FIRST POLICEMAN
SECOND POLICEMAN
JAILER
MILITARY DOCTOR
PRIEST
COMRADE

PROLOGUE

CHORUS: We are going to tell a war story, the true story of a time when one still had the duty to kill, for love of the Fatherland, other men whom one imagined loved a different Fatherland. Today, happily, Empire is served by mercenaries and bands of military rabble who feign no patriotic love . . .

FRIEND: Or only when they think of their retirement—but good private insurance is more effective, as we strongly advise them.

CHORUS: We are going to tell the story of a man who detested war to the point of mortifying his body and mutilating his own life, a man who declared war on war and who, driven by his passion, ended up nobly by killing it. It's the story of an act of resistance.

FRIEND: The unhappy result of a courageous choice—in those troubled times when only those who obeyed were worthy of honors and when deaths, millions of deaths, were considered a minor detail in the face of the Fatherland's glory. Hard times, let me tell you, I who, as you will soon see, don't stand out for having lived differently from the way that the majority of others lived—no, or only with a bit more decency and prudence instead of egotism, with realism rather than cowardice . . . But let's not exaggerate my modest virtues, this petty vulgarity of mine comes from a long practice of political militancy, and then, after all, militancy too is an effective way to avoid getting bored. Him, on the contrary, the man whose story we're going to tell, he was generous and resolute . . . and totally foreign to every political illusion.

CHORUS: Isn't political illusion quite often a lie? But no one is constrained to a lie.

FRIEND: Only resistance, disobedience, rebellion bear the name of truth.

CHORUS: The story happened in Italy during the Second World War. We are in a poor village in the northern part of the country: it's there that our friend, or our hero, or simply the tragic actor of a cruel era, lived deprived but happy with his wife. He works as a woodcutter. This is where he is called to arms, and this is where our story begins.

FRIEND: It's simply the story of a man who didn't want to make war. He succeeded at it through shrewdness and strength . . . But to what extent can one make war on war?

CHORUS: It's the story of thousands and thousands of men who are rebels, a swarm of freedom. In his pain, our man, first alone and then with others, swells the common life and gives it back the breath of difference.

FRIEND: But at the beginning, it's just the story of a man who didn't want to make war . . .

CHORUS: And you find that it's not enough? How many hypocrites have accused this little Machiavelli of desertion! What a desire for freedom was at the origin of his refusal! And what rebel potency was his! He remains a formidable example for generations to come.

FRIEND: Very well. As for me, I remember when he cried because he was no longer managing to survive . . . Such sadness he made us feel . . . And then why speak of him solely as a rebel who struggled against war? He was also a worker who didn't get on with the owner of the forest, he was a free man who detested the superstitious order of village life . . . Capitalist exploitation and the violence of the warlords, for him, were not much different.

CHORUS: All right. But you too, now, don't you transform him into an exception. Fighting against exploitation and fighting against war are the same, common sense shows us that both of them participate in the same idea. We know all about it, living under the boss's whip is not living. And poverty nourishes the desire to tear apart the network of powers everywhere and in whatever form it presents itself.

FRIEND: When terror besieges you and war threatens, the fearful soul is no less painful than the empty stomach. That's what I mean, and I would be grateful to you for taking it into account.

CHORUS: But let's get on with our story. It must be remembered that in this miserable village of woodcutters, at the time of our tale, there were of course the usual bosses, but there were also the King of Italy and the fascist Duce, and later the German Reich and the Nazi Duce. Between the first set and the second, there had actually been an armistice between the King and the Allies—this was in September 1943, and many of us really believed that we had finally obtained peace. Our man too . . .

FRIEND: Whatever they may be, all the regime changes did not make much difference for the people. Under fascism as under Nazism, it was difficult to find enough to eat; and to sit quietly in one's corner without having to declare one's faith in the Duce was impossible. And as for what is called thinking freely, you had to be very careful not to show it if you wanted to be left in peace—at the inn, there were plenty of spies. In short, at that time there was no freedom such as we have today, with all the television channels and the freedom of the press; and since we live well, we are all owners, right?

CHORUS: You will surely ask us why we are telling you such an old story. We are telling it to you because it's a story of war and fascism. And war never gets old, and we always find fascism and its cruelty on the horizon; and if everything changes with the centuries, war, fascism, and the vulgar violence of the bosses are always there: we are always entitled to them, we always end up stumbling over them. The captains' and sergeants' mustaches have changed, the techniques of persuasion and the ways of saying that exploitation is eternal have varied, the stupid cry of command that drives men to kill—or to produce—and that ends up leading them toward death, this cry is always the same.

FRIEND *(howling)*: *Eins, zwei,* to indicate the product, to communicate faster, perfect product, about-face, in play, *Feuer, Arbeit macht frei,* forward biscuit, *Gott mit uns,* Krupp, Agnelli, Pirelli, Peugeot, Michelin, *Achtung Banditen,* waiting for Stakhanovitch, *Achtung . . .*

CHORUS: Calm down. We are not only telling the story of a rebellion. It is also a geometrical demonstration that rebellion against war must lead, all together, to making war on war . . . by invoking at the same time our labor and nature, our common mother.

ACT I

A. The Decision

In the house. The **MAN** *rises from the bed. He picks up the letter that calls him to the front.*

MAN: So, my day has come. Today is Sunday. Yesterday evening they brought me the letter that calls me to arms. How did I manage to sleep last night? And yet my sleep was calm. I awoke only once, like

a sleepwalker, to piss. I'm calm because I had already decided. These
last months, I often posed the problem to myself, this letter must
arrive sooner or later. The war goes on. People talk only about that.
How many comrades in work have already gone? At the inn, on the
rare evenings when I happen to go there, there are ever fewer friends.
This war will be like the other one, when my father's brothers didn't
come back! This year, the priest postponed the gin rummy champion-
ship for the youngsters. Postponed until when? This war is not going
to end. It will be worse than the other one, when my father's brothers disappeared—no one knows where . . . Enough complaining, I'm
crying over my lot. Enough, I've decided, I'm not going to go . . . The
other day, when I gave the final blow to that fir tree that didn't want
to give up, I was stricken by doubt and emotion: wasn't I in the
process of killing it? No. Or maybe yes . . . But there, the struggle
was fair, there are many firs, we cut them down and they grow
back, nature is full of potency, every tree that I knock down with
my friends has given birth to thousands of others, every tree makes
a thousand spirits fly, swarms of life surround it. After knocking it
down, we have to cut it up—this trunk is a multitude of life experiences and rings that we read in the wood's cross section, as if it were
a hidden consciousness mysteriously engraved . . . Yes, that's how you
discover that nature is continually creating. Woodcutter's work is not
war. My work is part of the economy of nature. Here at home, we've
lived off the forest for thousands and thousands of years. They say
that our forest is one of the most beautiful in the world. Legend says
that it was here that the Venetian ships were made, the first to sail
the world's seas and invent an exodus for those who wanted to escape
from the bosses and the power of our villages.

 This letter I have in my hands: "Sir . . . the Fatherland . . . national
duty . . . the call . . . mobilization . . ." This letter is a letter of death.
As for me, a man and a woodcutter, I can't obey. My life never hesi-
tated to express itself as desire. Dying? No, that's not what I fear. The
cemetery recycles life. Killing? That's what I cannot do, kill someone
I don't know, someone who is a man like me, who is there before me
in a fog that doesn't allow you to know if you have killed him and
how. And then always the same question: why? I have no enemies.
My family has no enemies. My elders work peacefully. The only
enemy I have is the boss of the sawmill. He's always exploited us, he's

a fascist. Twenty years ago, he got the fascist squads to beat my father because he insisted on demanding a wage increase—for everyone—of course, the boss will never go off to be a soldier. His son claims that he's sick, calmly hidden away, the liar; but when violence becomes necessary, of course it's him that we'll find in front of us . . . cured, fascist, always underfoot. And so why doesn't he go? Because his work is in "the public interest"? And mine isn't? Why? That's not the problem. As for me, I'm not going off to war because I don't want to kill. I want to live, I want to love and procreate, like the bears that hide in the woods I want to hide myself too. But how? How can I refuse to present myself at the mobilization? The police and the fascists will come looking for me. These cops are a murderous wind that crushes the bones. They'll beat me: "Traitor to the Fatherland, coward." They'll threaten to kill me. How can I refuse to go? How can I win in refusing?

I remember one night when we were hunting. We had gone very high up, to the edge of the glacier. There were mountain goats, we surprised them because we had walked against the wind, which had blocked our scent and its threat. When it saw us and understood that it couldn't get away, the largest of them, in order to defend the others—the young, the female—drew itself up to its full size. Its body was an obstacle to the massacre. We didn't shoot, we could have killed all of them at once, we couldn't do it, what kind of hunt would that have been? But why am I thinking about those wild beasts now? As for me, in order to oppose the war, I do not follow my instinct; and my refusal to make war is rational. As for me, I consider only human resistance as strong, I oppose the reason of peace to the violence of war.

How often the trees respond to the force of the wind by bending. The branches curve in order not to break, and that's how they prepare for resistance. Bending to resist the wind . . . I want to draw myself up to my full size like an animal amid the mountain rocks, I want to transform myself into a pack, wildly, to defend myself . . . or curve myself like a tree from our woods, twist my body like a branch that opposes the intelligence of its live nerves to the wind. Several months ago, when I fell off the mule and my back seemed broken, I made myself a promise: no, I will not report to the recruiting office, no, I will not do it, and when they come looking for me, I will bend myself double, I will be like a tree stubbornly twisted to the order of destruction, a twisted tree that stops the violence of the winds and the storm, and that shakes and trembles in unison with the seasons and tempos of life . . . The war will not have me, the potentates of destruction will not have me . . .

(He reflects further.)

I would like to be lucid . . . I'm not managing it . . . generous with myself . . . I'm not managing it. This war is like a volcano that absorbs and sets fire to everything . . . all of us logs will be thrown into the furnace . . . this story has no meaning . . .

. . . I am poor. If I manage to survive, will this war make me richer? No. My poverty will be the same, the bosses will be the same. And then? What injunction drives me to climb aboard a fully marked destiny? No—as for me, I want to love. They tell me that my choice is anarchist. But them, what order do they offer me? They say that my refusal is egoistic. But them, what community do they offer? Me, I'm collective. I would like to drive a train, and all my friends would join me, would fill it, would hang on outside and on top. I would like to feed the furnace that runs on desire and peace, a train full of all the men who want peace . . . It whistles in the night, my train, in these days of war, in the fog of consciences broken into a thousand pieces . . .

No, I'm here, I'm waiting for a new day to break. I can only ground my will on myself, I must oblige my love of others to detest myself, my body to become the painful instrument of my desire for freedom. I can only count on myself, because my hatred of war makes my love of the world solitary . . .

Everything in its own time. I resist, I differ with myself, tomorrow hope will be reborn . . . Can the bent tree ever stand up straight? Will my spirit still have the necessary energy? The village elders always point out a big tree, up there above us. It was a big bent tree. One day, an avalanche hurtled toward the village—it was the first time that happened, and also the last—but the avalanche was cut in two, broken into pieces and scattered by the big twisted tree. And when the snow finished melting, the tree was straight.

B. The Man Bends

In the house. His **WIFE** *enters.*

WIFE: Where are you? Why are you sitting in the dark?

MAN: Some thoughts. Delirium. I'm deciding. Yesterday evening, they brought me this accursed letter that I was waiting for . . .

(The woman cries.)

Don't cry. Don't cry. It's good that you've come, today is Sunday, we have all day to argue . . .

WIFE: But what do you want to argue about!

(She sobs.)

I know, you always say that you don't want to kill. But are you really anxious to be shot right away? That's how they punish desertion in time of war.

MAN: No, I don't want to be shot. I'm thinking that there are a thousand ways to avoid going off to war. I can cut off a finger, shoot myself in the foot, or even get a comrade to break an arm by slamming shut the train door . . .

WIFE: No, you'll make yourself sick . . .

MAN: That's not the problem. The problem instead is if I do that, the pigs will find a way to punish me all the same. When my father returned from the war, sad as a dog, he told me that self-mutilation was punished as if it were sedition. My decision is different: a physical problem that is also psychic, a bodily accident that shows my refusal to be madness . . .

WIFE: My love, you'll make yourself sick! I don't want your body to suffer. My life is dedicated to your joy just as your body is dedicated to my pleasure.

MAN: It's not my body but my head that must act. Tonight, through the hours, I've reviewed all the possibilities of flight and all the ruses . . . I've weighed their strength realistically. Alone, it's difficult, it's impossible to resist the laws and their violence. One can no longer seek refuge in the forest like savages. Hunger and cold strip you naked, deliver you into their abject hands like a sacrificial beast. Enough of these dreams. In these conditions, to resist means to give proof of shrewdness . . .

WIFE: But you, you are naive, solid, and straightforward . . . I love you for that simplicity of yours, for your directness and strength . . . You are a crystal that they will break under the soles of their boots . . . No, my love, you must be prudent . . .

MAN: Sly like a dove . . .

WIFE: What do you mean?

MAN: I mean that I will submit to their will like a lunatic. I am ready to suffer in order to fool them, to nourish my hatred in silence, to martyr my body in order to sabotage their war, and to submit to their control in order to destroy their discipline and infringe their laws. I will do anything to desert.

WIFE: Those are political slogans . . . the exclamations of an idealist who doesn't know the grammar of life . . .

MAN: No, my sweet beloved, that's not so. I have studied the movements of the trees that resist the violence of nature, and the animals that defend themselves from the violence of men. They curl up, they curve. In order to resist, they bend, they have the strength of a divine ruse. That's what I'm going to do . . . Don't be surprised, don't let yourself be overcome with fear. These are certain movements that nature has taught me . . .

(He begins to twist, to bend, as if he were looking for an improbable, almost impossible, silhouette: bent but firm.)

The fascists always say: I break, but I don't bend. As for me, I bend in order not to break. This is how I will await the hour of revolt. This is how my hatred, by sacrificing itself, will be victorious . . .

WIFE: Stop, you are mad . . .

(The MAN is now bent at a right angle. Then he straightens up. They sit down on the bed.)

You are mad.

MAN: A little. A little mad. Nothing serious. The means is adequate to the end. Look at me: I promise you that, thanks to this bent spine, I will manage to keep my life in a straight line, to affirm my desire for peace! Bent at a right angle! Will I succeed? My beautiful love, say yes. Certain trees that I know are like this . . . magnificent, dramatic . . . curved, curled up to defend peace, to defend life, I will manage it . . .

WIFE: Calm down, go slowly, don't move too much, stay quiet here next to me. My love, come toward the center of the bed. I'm going to embrace you until your body becomes straight again. On the bed, stretched out beside my body, on my body, under my body, at my side . . . My love, my hands want to caress you from head to foot, tall and straight like you are now, my fingers will follow the line of all your curves and the harmony of your strength . . .

MAN: I promise you that I will remain straight every night at your side, to love you. Even if I bend every day in order to disobey the laws and to respect the honor of humanity.

WIFE: You will not manage it . . .

(She sobs lovingly.)

My God, how will you do it? They will say that the bent man no longer makes love to me because he's not capable of it. I will have to defend myself from men who will swarm around me like fastidious flies. I will do it willingly . . . But are you being serious when you say that every night you will be tall and straight, and you will treat me like a wife, like your wife? My love, is that it?

MAN: I will manage it. We will manage it. We are going to need a lot of strength and a lot of irony. I love you.

(He rises and comically apes the bent man. They laugh.)

(Blackout)

C. The Police

In the house. Monday morning. A knock at the door. The **WIFE** *rises from the bed, puts on a robe, and goes to the door.*

VOICES *(The police)*: Open up.

WIFE: Who is it?

VOICES: The police!

(The **WIFE** *opens the door. The* **POLICE** *enter. The* **MAN** *is in bed.)*

FIRST POLICEMAN: Haven't you received the letter of induction? Why haven't you reported at the barracks at dawn?

SECOND POLICEMAN: There are bad rumors going around about your lack of patriotism. I know your family—of course, they're not fascists, but they've always done their duty. As for me, I like you well enough: if you didn't report this morning, as the letter ordered, it's surely because you're ill, is that it?

MAN: I'm really sick. The Fatherland will pardon me, but I can't manage to rise. I've tried. Ask my wife. But my back won't allow it.

FIRST POLICEMAN: What kind of story is this? Up until Friday, you were in the mountains cutting down trees!

MAN: You, the trees, you never cut them down, and the forest, you don't know what it is. That's why you don't have the rheumatism that I have. My father died of arthritis too.

SECOND POLICEMAN: Your father died like a drunkard, and it was only thanks to me that he avoided prison. He always spoke ill of the Duce and said that the King never worked.

MAN: My father was killed by work. You've never done anything in life, you've worked even less than the King . . . Stop showing off, parasite, slacker . . . Thank heaven that I have rheumatism . . .

FIRST POLICEMAN: If you keep it up, I'll arrest you.

SECOND POLICEMAN: Calm down!

(*In a low voice to the* **FIRST POLICEMAN**)

Calm down! Outside there are already people protesting. The woodcutter is well known and esteemed. This is a village of savages, smugglers, hunters, and con men.

(*To the* **WIFE**)

Calm down. Didn't you call the doctor? And couldn't you offer us a coffee? I'm really getting the impression that we'll have to carry your man to the barracks.

WIFE: Yeah, I went to inform the doctor. He asked me why he had to come, and when I told him, he shrugged his shoulders. They say that there are many who fall ill when the call to arms arrives. And in any case, I don't have any coffee to offer you.

MAN *(changing his tone)*: You know, rheumatism is dirty trick, it comes when you least expect it. It blocks you up. It's already happened to me other times . . . It's an occupational hazard. There are even professors who come to the woods to study our illness . . . They've studied it: brave people, it was to avoid paying us health insurance . . .

SECOND POLICEMAN: Here's my fatherly advice: come with us to the barracks. The military doctor will see if you are sick . . . Like your wife says, there are many who don't want to serve the Fatherland. But later, they change their tune.

WIFE: I see that you are up to date with the bad feelings of some . . . Is it true that last week you had to chase after drunken soldiers who had scattered into the city and who didn't want to get back on the trains heading for Russia?

FIRST POLICEMAN: That's defeatist talk. That's enough.

WIFE: Pardon. It was a whore who told me that. The soldiers had tied her to the rails in order to prevent the train from leaving . . .

MAN: That's enough, that's enough. Help me get up.

The **POLICEMEN** *and the* **WIFE** *get the* **MAN** *out of bed. They straighten him up, but he bends at a right angle . . . at first slowly, then more and more quickly. The* **POLICEMEN** *look at him, stupefied, then try to straighten him. The entire scene resembles a kind of ballet.*

FIRST POLICEMAN: Stand up straight: love of the Fatherland cannot bow down before rheumatism.

SECOND POLICEMAN: If you're not mocking us, the doctor will help you.

WIFE: My love, are you sick? How can I help you?

MAN: I can't manage to stay upright. Pain bends me like a tree before the wind, like a frightened mountain goat.

FIRST POLICEMAN *(in a low voice)*: The Duce is leading us to victory.

SECOND POLICEMAN *(in a low voice)*: This is one shitty job . . . but at least I'm not going to Russia.

WIFE *(in a low voice)*: How beautiful you are, my husband!

MAN *(in a low voice)*: How I love you, my beautiful one!

The **POLICEMEN** *lift the* **MAN** *onto their shoulders with difficulty and, after leaving, head toward the barracks. The* **WIFE** *cries.*

ACT II

A. Prison Life: The Doctor

In a cell. The **MAN** *is constantly bent.*

JAILER: Straighten up, the doctor's here.

MAN: Help me. I can't manage it. I'm completely stunned. Yesterday evening they gave me an injection of I don't know what, to calm me down . . . That's what they said among themselves . . . it made them laugh.

JAILER: That's enough. They can kill you if they want. I've seen them do it, men who showed off . . . I'm going to help you, I knew that old alcoholic who was your father, the medicine cures the sick but kills those who are healthy . . . How much of that I've seen, those like you who shammed and who left here genuinely mad . . . It's in your best interests to make a rational compromise . . .

While the **JAILER** *helps the Bent* **MAN** *to rise, we hear an enormous noise like an explosion . . . The* **JAILER** *jumps, terrorized; the Bent* **MAN** *doesn't flinch . . .*

MILITARY DOCTOR *(behind the door, before entering)*: I've observed him, I haven't seen the faker react. It's odd. There's no doubt that he is a faker. After that horse-size dose that we injected into him, he no longer has any psychic defenses; he's been subjected to the loud noise test, I've quite clearly seen that he had no reaction, but that's his case. The situation must be forced . . . He hasn't budged . . . it's really bizarre!

(He enters. To the **JAILER***)*

Hand me the steel bar.

JAILER: Here you are.

The **JAILER** *and the* **DOCTOR** *tie the Bent* **MAN** *to a flexible steel bar. The* **MAN** *straightens up. Then, when they detach it, he bends again. This ballet can continue as long as desired.*

MILITARY DOCTOR: Let's attach it, let's straighten him . . .

JAILER: I can't do any better. This man is mad. We will never be able to straighten him. Madness doesn't look after itself . . .

MILITARY DOCTOR: Once again . . . It's not possible for him to bend yet again. I've never seen a madman like him . . . He's a one-hundred-percent faker. In the big book of military medicine, there's a list of tests for debunking a fake . . . It's a genuine science . . . But then why doesn't this man straighten up?

JAILER: They asked me to set a ferocious dog on him. I did it. No one ran. The Man didn't budge. The dog went and lay down peacefully at his feet.

MILITARY DOCTOR: Why doesn't science know how to correct slackers? The Fatherland is made up of healthy men and warriors . . . Why has this man been reduced to this monstrous state?

The doctor exits.

MAN: I'm counting sheep, five thousand sheep, backwards. Always. I never stop counting them. Four thousand nine hundred ninety-nine. Four thousand nine hundred ninety-eight. Four thousand nine hundred ninety-seven . . . Sheep who run away by jumping over the fences . . . Four thousand nine hundred ninety-six: there's a soldier who escapes from the train that's heading to Russia. The sheep flees the butcher, the soldier flees the glory. Four thousand nine hundred ninety-five . . . I'm falling asleep . . . I would like so much to sleep . . .

(He almost falls asleep, and raves.)

"Quiet, quiet, you're keeping me awake . . . Talk softer . . . If I could sleep, I might make love. I'd go into the woods. My eyes would see . . . the sky, the earth. I'd run, run, they wouldn't catch me . . . Nature! . . . There's something dripping in my head . . . A heart, a heart in my head."[1]

JAILER: I give you milk: you lap it up like a dog. I give you pasta: you eat it like a pig . . . I'm beginning to believe that your madness is real . . . but then your suffering must be unendurable . . .

MAN: This prison reeks of suffering. You don't see it, you don't hear it, the contaminated, asthmatic, difficult, painful breathing all through the night? You don't perceive it, the veil of sweat and fear all through the days? In places like this, madness is raised to the second power, and only the crazy survive.

The **MILITARY DOCTOR** *enters the room and gives the* **MAN** *a new injection.*

MILITARY DOCTOR: Here's one that should make you more docile.

MAN: More docile than what? Doctor, you will never be able to understand to what extent the weakness of the suffering man is a strength. Your medicines will never constrain the soul to obedience . . . any more than they will straighten my spine to send me into combat . . .

(He sings to himself.)

Mean medicine, science of power . . .

Will you ever be able, doctor, to contain the rivers of pain that flow through the world? And the rancid and poisonous river that gushes out of this prison? Everything is absurd here, and me, evidently I am no less mad than you are.

MILITARY DOCTOR: Jailer, put our man into quarantine. Keep him under permanent watch. Inspect to see if he straightens up. Perhaps he is truly mad . . .

(He laughs alone.)

But even the mad can't refuse to die for the Fatherland! Otherwise, where will we find the heroes?

(To the **MAN**)

In any case, if you go on like that, no one will ever be able to get you out of this business by pronouncing the magic word "discharged."

MAN: "Discharged"? From now on, who will be able to discharge the intimate knowledge of my life's pain?

(Pause. The **DOCTOR** *exits. Then the* **MAN** *starts to moan, alone.)*

Four thousand nine hundred ninety-four, four thousand nine hundred ninety-three . . . Sheep, soldiers who flee from the moments of life that find no rest . . . my wife lost in the infinity of this void . . .

(Pause. He moans. He curls up under the blanket, bent over himself.)

You will never manage it, doctor. There is light . . . some- where . . . and I am grasping it, like when, in the forest, I warmed my face in it . . . filthy bosses' science . . . like the mountain goat said to the hunter who took aim at him . . .

B. Prison Life: The Priest

Prison. Cell. The **MAN** *is constantly bent. Enter a* **PRIEST**.

PRIEST: My brother, you are suffering. Can I help you? We must all bend down before God, but by the grace of God, we can be straight and faithful soldiers of the Lord, the Fatherland, and our honor.

MAN: I thank you, my Father. I have been locked up here for days and days, and my back aches, and my body is tense. I no longer feel pleasure. If you jack me off, perhaps I will straighten up, like a good soldier.

PRIEST: Don't swear . . . Your wife, who came looking for me, has been very nice. I promised her news of you.

MAN: Forgive me, Priest. I have been locked up here for days and days, and I've lost my head. If you stick a finger up my ass, perhaps I will straighten up, like a good soldier.

PRIEST: Your wife would not allow such vulgarities. She is very attached to you, she is the Wife of the Man you are. She is doing everything to free you. She is generous and sad . . . and though she is tied to you by the sacred bonds of marriage, with others, she is open and generous; and she lets the servants of the Fatherland and the Church divine her capacity to love in order to help you and to bring you out of the difficulties in which you find yourself . . . She suggests that you give in a little.

MAN: You too have fallen under the spell, Priest? Speak no more of my wife. In the end I could accept that she survives by acting as a whore, even though I would be extremely sad about it, but I will not tolerate that she polished a pipe for you for free.

PRIEST: That's enough, stop playing at madness. Vulgarity won't help you to free yourself from your destiny . . . For the last time, I ask you to listen to me . . . I can help you . . . You have sinned against the law and the state, against the faith and the divine mystery. Our fascist country is struggling against a great enemy of religion. Each person must support this war effort. You, you didn't want to do it, you have sinned. But I am ready to open the way to God's pardon, the King's pardon, and the Fatherland's pardon. You must recognize your errors and redress them . . . The Virgin will help you.

MAN: I thank you, Priest. Tonight, I made love with the Virgin; and Christ congratulated me because I have a body that is more capable than his of bearing the cross . . . I don't need you to speak with God. I talk best with him through my fellow men—we, God and I, we want peace. You are not the one, Priest, who will succeed in convincing me of the holy war.

PRIEST: I came to see you in gentleness; my measured reproach for you was mixed with a certain admiration for your strength of spirit . . . but your injuries are those of a madman or a delinquent . . . All that remains for me to tell you is: repent!

MAN: Priest, I'm looking at you from below. From below, one sees the world differently than those who see it from above . . . From below, man sees more justly than God . . . the bent body feels more true than the straight body . . . Christ is holier than God, the cross is not high but low and curved toward the earth . . . Madness is no more credible than reason, but it certainly knows more than reason . . . Sometimes, actually, it is revealed as love . . . Priest, you have confused what you should not confuse: my disobedience and the generosity of my wife, my resistance and the stupid conviction that the bosses and the cops have served the Fatherland even though they are betraying it . . . My pain cannot be understood through pity . . . that would be true madness . . . It's you, Priest, who are mad, not me. I am only asking to live and to love, I refuse this community that religion organizes into castration and masochism. You speak by pretending to pray . . . but this prayer leaves the mouth dry and desperate . . . You, Priest, could you ever imagine what the love of life is?

PRIEST: Listen, man, I don't even intend to react to your delirious blasphemies. As for me, I'm an agent of the Church. The popes have always exalted just war in defense of religion; and for a century they have always expressed themselves in favor of holy war and against socialism . . . When you choose to desert, when you sabotage the common effort to contain and battle communism, not only have you sinned, but you present yourself before the human arm of the supreme law as a subversive . . . I wanted to help you. I must not do so. And if I ever do, it will only be because your wife is beautiful and convincing . . .

MAN: Go away, Priest, I could kill you.

(*He straightens up. The* **PRIEST** *exits, struck by fear. Pause. The* **MAN** *reflects.*)

Stop. Bend yourself. Be calm. You are sick, not mad. Arthritis does not ease the blows of anger and it does not permit violence . . . But then, how can I express my indignation in the face of these charlatans selling smoke and mirrors, in the face of these forgers of superstitions? The war and the fascist massacres destroy all the credibility of these wild men of pity. Why is prison a place where their hypocrisy still finds something to sell? If Christ wanted to return to Earth, it's here, in the prison, that he would begin to preach again, against the priests and against war. Be calm. Bend yourself. The moment to straighten yourself up has not yet come.

C. Prison Life: Discussion

The **MAN** *is constantly bent.*

FRIEND (*entering the cell*): Hello . . . I well knew that I would meet you . . . When the policemen came to get me because I hadn't presented myself at the induction, they told me laughingly, "You're not going to make us sweat like that other coward who's bent in two"!

MAN: Hello, how are you? How long have you been here? Have you seen my wife? Here, you forget the passing days . . . Time is marked only by resistance . . . Talk to me, tell me . . .

FRIEND: You see, Man, in reality I am not here because I refused to go off to war. Everyone knows that I'm sick, and that death's strong wind is blowing on my shoulders. No, they've thrown me in prison because I'm antifascist. I detest their wooden language, their cock-and-bull stories, their corruption. And then I also like to eat well and speak ill of power. When you look good, you drink and play the lottery, and when you're lucky enough to have a few coins in your pocket, they don't even think of denouncing you as subversive . . . They look for communists among the poor . . . But me, I do the opposite, I look for communists everywhere . . . Always prudently, with much circumspection . . . Except for them, what can you expect to do with them, they don't appreciate paradox and irony . . . So there you have the reason why I'm here. They came for me yesterday . . . I was in the middle of preparing a bomb . . . They caught me in the act . . . They were shocked.

Yes, I've seen your wife. You can be proud of her. Beautiful as she is, all the bosses and all the fascists and all the priests are courting her, but she remains inaccessible as only a rebel woman knows how to be—or wants to be—and as your love demands . . .

MAN: Alas, here love gets forgotten . . . and the rest too. Me, I can't stay upright, you twist yourself with hunger and hatred . . . "Every man his speciality."[2]

FRIEND: Alas, it's true, comrade, here hatred begins to burn again.

MAN: But why must this violence and this rage span the world? War lacerates social links, and transforms us into enemies . . . And yet, in the horrible misery of this cell in which I live, I sometimes get the sense that I'm being protected. If it were only the desire for my wife, I would tell myself: be calm in prison, bend yourself further in order not to break. Here, there is an infinitesimal refuge, a hideout, a lair that's impossible to reach, and yet so potent for resisting . . .

FRIEND: Sickness and disdain are destroying my body: I understand your desire for peace, but as for me, I no longer want to have these filthy fascists always in front of me . . . I'd like to be able to eat, and not to cough, drink, smoke, and spit from the violence and contempt against these violent corrupters of humanity . . .

MAN: But why isn't it possible to live a life that would have freedom as its goal? A life in which neither the state nor any other authority would be instituted to impose fear, war, and the wrath of God on the citizen . . . Where, on the contrary, they would be set up in order to liberate the citizen from fear and to permit him freedom and joy in total safety, without doing evil to others . . . Why isn't that possible? Why do we not succeed in escaping this solitude in which we have taken refuge, why can't we construct a common freedom?

FRIEND: Let's laugh as much as we still can! Man, today it's capitalism in its fascist forms. If they don't succeed in rendering you alone and miserable, they transform you into a lonely and desperate prisoner all the same. In the old days, there was the feudal fiefdom: since then, for us, nothing much has changed . . . The bosses want to eat all the cake . . . you know it very well . . . Our woods are among the most beautiful and the richest in the Alps . . . And it's always the same ones who are the owners, and the priests, and the policemen there? Long live the fiefdoms, long live Capital and fascism, they are eternal, my friend, let's kneel and pray that they give us something to eat . . .

(Pause)

. . . or let's construct a cataclysm that destroys them . . .

MAN: The cataclysm is already at work. The earth trembles and the multitudes arise . . . Me, I am a poor woodcutter, my voice is as low as the rustling of a leaf. But when all the leaves of the big tree murmur, then it's a concert, a swarm of sounds and force . . . You see, my friend, ever since this war got bogged down in the long haul, the fascists are feeling the anticipatory signs of defeat . . . and as for me, I've got the notion that the music of resistance is no longer made up only of the wind that shakes the trees, but also the leaves that invent new sounds for nature . . . These are the sounds that we hear today . . .

FRIEND: So, let's organize. I am fat, I love life and above all food, but I am first and foremost a militant. Libertarian? Of course, but perhaps also communist. Did you know that? They suspected it, I'm the one who told you . . . Let's organize, then, let's help the hurricane to blow, to expand, to reproduce itself in our consciousnesses . . .

(He reflects.)

I am trying to lead a beautiful life because that's a condition for struggling. Good taste and pleasure are not sad things, they construct a practical intelligence through the body's well-being . . .

(Pause)

But how serious I am! It's ridiculous, here, in prison, you bent in two and me listening to the wheezing of tuberculosis that is hollowing out my bones . . . There is something comical in inventing an organization for ourselves, in speaking of communism, as we hang on with such difficulty . . . Don't you get the feeling that we are truly mad?

MAN: Call it madness, if you want . . . But the new world knows only resistance . . . When I bend in order to avoid accepting the rules of their authority, I am destroying the foundations, I am insulting their legitimacy—I am sawing through the support beam of their power . . . When they look at me and analyze me, there are those who feel themselves offended, or worse, insulted . . . There is rage in the face of my madness, a ferocious rage as if they found themselves faced with an act of revolt . . . Cretins, don't you understand that it's exactly that?

FRIEND: How many times I've wanted to laugh—and everyone heard me do it in the village—at the great demonstrations of weakling arrogance and the inconsistent exhibitions of power! The chief fascist passed self-importantly before the inn, and yet he envied our din . . . but if he entered, silence reigned . . . How many times have the stupid faces of the Italian Duce and his German buddy, how many times have these portraits attached to the walls like flyspecks made me snicker . . . But I had forgotten that their violence transforms us: when we are subjected to it, we feel a deep wound in the soul, and life becomes sad when history is marked by death . . . Then the mad laughter is turned into sobbing . . . It's like when you don't eat: you get thin and become miserable.

MAN: Bending in order not to break is difficult, it's painful— but I detest them because they are war . . . the bosses, the fascists . . . destruction and hunger . . . bending in order not to break . . . it's necessary . . .

(He reflects.)

But this is not simply a moment, a defense . . . No, it's quite different, my friend, we, we are a cataclysm . . . against power . . . organizing the war on war . . . when will this be possible?

ACT III

A. The War Is Over

In the village square. September 8, 1943. The **MAN** *is upright, he has straightened up.*

MAN: Tonight, the jailer threw me out in front of the prison . . . He howled: "The war is over" . . . I had trouble believing that it was true, and yet it is . . . I heard it on the radio . . . even the police seemed happy, the fascists have disappeared . . . The priests intoned their timid Te Deums without ringing the bells . . . Then, in one blow, I straightened up . . . It almost made me ill, I breathed deeply . . . The jailer looked at me as if I were the devil . . . There are so many people dancing here, there is so much happiness . . . I'm moving ahead painfully, awaiting I don't know what, perhaps an infinite joy . . . or further tragedies?

The **WIFE** *enters, sees him upright. They find one another in silence. Music. They dance. At first he is rather stiff; then, as the dance goes on, he loosens up.*

WIFE: My love, last night I dreamed that you were in my bed . . . I felt you inside me . . . but you couldn't come and take me because you were still constantly bent in two . . . and me, I asked in my dream why there must be war between my front and my rear . . .

(She laughs.)

Forgive me, I am saying just anything. Now I have the whole of you, beautiful as a god, once again . . .

The **FRIEND** *enters. The three of them embrace.*

FRIEND: First they put you outside. And then the fascist, the prison boss, arrived and told me, "You've won, accursed communists . . . Go on, then, but I would have liked to kill you . . ." I didn't understand at all, I must admit to you that I was afraid: he had the face of a rabid dog, I didn't reply at all, I left running, I was really flying . . . And then outside there were so many people making merry that I remained gripped by it . . . And then I looked for something to eat: I didn't have any notion that peace had brought with it a lot of polenta or salami . . . Well, someone, an angel, made me a beautiful goulash, a miracle. And now, the miracles are multiplying: I see you standing upright . . .

(He is struck by a fit of coughing.)

. . . . hell of a rogue, me too, I believed for a while that you were curved for real, bent at a right angle . . . Your resistance . . . ha ha . . .

(He laughs noisily.)

. . . your insulting body, its disdain, your madness . . . your heroism— and who will ever succeed in separating them . . . As potent as it is, the body that resists . . . this is what ended the war . . .

WIFE: Listen, my friends, don't be stupid. Your philosophy and your coughing don't go with the joy of this multitude . . . On the other hand, we don't understand a large part of what is going on, peace and quiet is still hypothetical, and our joy is open to the dark possibility of a new war . . . Danger is quite near . . . I feel it passing through my body . . . I have just embraced my husband again, but my senses are still those of a ferocious beast defending its brood . . .

(Noises are heard.)

VOICES: They've found the police chief, he was hanged there, in front of the barracks . . .

VOICES: They say that the forest boss was rescued . . . The woodcutters have sacked his house . . .

The fascists' chief has barricaded himself inside the city hall . . . The poachers fired their carbines at the windows . . .

(Pause)

WIFE: The impossibility of forgetting acts of violence endured, and the weight of the dead that the war imposed, and the horrible things for which the fascists are responsible, and the hatred, and the vengeance, all that seems to be corrupting the air . . .

(Pause)

But we are here now: let's dance, let's take the sugar in the boss's cabinets and larders, and the coffee in the army depots, and the brandy in the fascists' penthouses, and the wine in the priests' cellars . . . Let's drink, let's dance, let's make love . . .

(Addressing the **FRIEND**.*)*

You didn't say that man lives on goulash . . .

(Addressing her husband, full of innuendo.)

But not on that alone . . . my beautiful man, I desire you . . .

The people's ball continues, the music too.

Let's dance, let's drink, let's make love. Right now. Our tomorrows are dark. Courage, let's entertain ourselves . . . And if you want to keep doing philosophy, if this unexpected freedom stuns you, I am giving you an order to be joyful. I will be your new jailer, I will compel you to enthusiasm for freedom . . . So, let's drink some good wine! Some gaiety! Because all that gives us strength for the struggles to come.

(To her husband)

Tonight, you must make me a child.

B. The War Goes On

In the village square. The square is empty. Silence.

FRIEND: The Nazis are about to arrive . . . The fascists are re-organizing and heading toward the village . . . They've set fire to the church by the cemetery, and now they are coming up toward the Castle from the side, they are coming toward us from below . . . They say that they must retake control of the village because this is where the roads toward the plain begin.

MAN *(He reflects.)*: We must resist . . .

While the **FRIEND** *nods yes and circulates around the square discussing with various people, the* **MAN** *isolates himself to reflect.*

Resist? We must defend, kill. What is happening in my head? Defending oneself against war cannot mean making war . . . Refusing to kill cannot imply having to kill . . . Why does it go this way? Why can defending life be transformed into imposing war? There is no choice. The fascists are the ones who impose it on us . . . The tree must straighten up . . . This is against nature, it's impossible that I should succeed . . . The miracle of the bent tree that stopped the avalanche, the one of which the village elders tell, will it repeat itself? That's enough, we must resist. This time we will be the avalanche . . .

Enter the **WIFE**.

WIFE: What are you doing? Everyone is reflecting on what must be done against the fascists and the Nazis who are coming up the valley . . . My belly bears your son . . . It tells me that we must resist . . . We can no longer bend. This potent little animal that I'm carrying inside me is life, it's our justice.

MAN: Defending life . . . Of course . . . But in this decision of ours, don't you feel the contamination of hatred and corruption?

WIFE: Man, I loved you when you were bent. But today I am the one who is bent over my maternal belly. I defended you when you were bent. But today, I ask you to defend this common which is ours and which, bent over itself, trembles and straightens in my belly. It's not a matter of killing but of giving a body to desire, and joy to life.

They embrace.

MAN *(as they emerge from their embrace)*: We are going to stop them with the potency of an avalanche . . . I love you . . .

The **WIFE** *exits.*

MAN *(starting to howl)*: We must resist.

Confusion. Then silence.

FRIEND: We have no weapons.

MAN: Look down there, in the square, beside the inn. There is a guard passing by, he's armed. Give me your pipe.

He slips to the other end of the square and presses the pipe into the guard's back.

MAN *(to the guard)*: If you don't give me your weapon, I'll kill you.

He takes the weapon, the guard flees.

MAN *(to the* **FRIEND***)*: And there's the first weapon . . . Demand the others from thieves, deserters, hunters, slackers . . . And right now, ring the bells, warn everyone that we're going to have to resist . . . or flee . . . The fascists are returning . . .

(Pause. The light changes. The bells ring. The **MAN** *remains alone.)*

What's happening? Why is the war going on? How is it possible that history plays such horrible tricks on us? Why is the very name of peace in doubt? Here's the scandalous spectacle of someone who struggled with all his strength for peace, and who now finds himself having to make war once again . . . to be straight . . . He is just as much a rebel as when he was bent. A little time passes and the scandal grows in my own body, and in my conscience . . . My will, the decision about what I must do, all this is undermined by doubt. I am suffering as a result of events that I didn't think I had to revisit—life, love, hope must now be at stake in the uncertain conflict that opposes us to an enemy who is ever more invasive and murderous. Why? Help me, spirits of the forest . . . Help me, my son, you who wail in that lagoon of love that is your mother's belly!

(Pause)

Oh! Here comes our Friend.

FRIEND: Many have already taken up arms. Some comrades, some inhabitants of the valley, some inhabitants of the towns . . . There are also many soldiers who are deserting and rebelling against the order to return to the barracks . . . but the Nazis and fascists are coming up the valleys—they most surely are! They are seeking to block the mountain passes in order to allow their army to reorganize . . . For them, we are bandits . . . It's like in Russia, they want to kill all the rebels . . .

(*Pause. First talking to himself, then gradually again to the* **MAN**.)

I am already tired of this story. I want to sit down at a table to have
a good goulash. These last days, these last hours, my lungs have
brought me back to reality several times, and with a certain insis-
tence. And then: what is to be done? How to make it say: we are no
longer resisting, the situation is desperate, we are no longer organizing because there is too little time . . . How to say this while everything is conspiring so that life can no longer express itself except by
rebelling and armed resisting? Man, I am a communist, but I swear
to you that often I don't understand at all why communism and war
are forced into such an unnatural alliance.

MAN: I am sticking to it, to communism. We must defend ourselves.
We must defend our common. Of course the strength of our common
is undermined by doubt, the discussion is always open, the utopia of
a happy life is shrinking from day to day, almost humiliating us, in
order to be able to come true. My master woodcutter told me that
happiness is a thing that is never realized, but it survives in the form
of an ever-stronger and vaster desire . . . When I asked my father,
who was a drunkard, what happiness meant, he answered that it
was a word that could only be pronounced while drinking a glass in
order to make a migraine go away . . . Who knows if all these people
around us want to struggle? . . . But here, we must arm ourselves
against the fascists and the bosses . . . As for us, we hate war and
we're afraid . . . We are constrained to war . . . My father told me
often that happiness is a dream, and that to embody it demands intelligence: olives too need a good wine in order to be digested . . . How
did we make these woods that belong to us answer the bosses . . . We
had to use force . . . but force is repugnant . . . And now what do
we do when faced with these Nazis and fascists who want us dead?
Why are we obliged to make war, we who were granted freedom by
becoming impotent, curved, and bent, why are we obliged to become
heroes? Why us, who desire work and wealth, why are we forced to
destroy? . . .

I tremble at it, my friend, but we cannot refuse this terrible twist of
fate.

Pause. The light changes. Evening falls.

FRIEND (*addressing the* **MAN**): Yes, sir, comrade commandant! Give me the order to send out for goulash! I pray you. My stomach is trembling, while my lungs are torn with coughing . . . If I had always eaten goulash, my lungs would be intact . . . Without goulash, death is coming . . .

(in a low voice)

What the doctor doesn't say, the stomach affirms . . .

(in a loud voice, addressing the **MAN** *once more)*

Yes, sir, comrade . . . We are a hundred, we are two hundred, we are many with weapons, the enemy is approaching . . . the comrades are blocking the mountain paths . . . we have set mines and the defense is ready . . . you could say that a people's army is born . . .

He snickers.

MAN (*ironically*): Good . . . Bravo, you don't know what joy this gives me . . . So let's demand this sacred goulash . . . We have all become generals, colonels, and majors, this must not be as difficult as all that . . . My wife will prepare it for us, okay? Long live goulash . . . but perhaps we no longer have time . . .

(We hear a clamor, not of festivity but of agitation, action . . . an active and joyful break.)

My friend, after we have finished not eating our goulash—the gods are conspiring against us—we will tell the whole world that our army, which is forming so rapidly, must also dissolve just as rapidly . . . Every comrade, with his own weapons, will have to construct guerrilla groups that are as effective as they are small, free, and unpredictable . . . Let's attack the enemy by surprise, let's break his supply lines, let's interfere with his lines of communication . . . And, above all, let's avoid the illusion of fighting like an army would . . . Our war is a war against war, a war against all armies . . . Factories of destruction, violence of command . . . There is no reason to have a command, a goal is enough for us: freedom, the common happiness.

FRIEND: I have always thought that communism meant goulash, freedom, and . . . further, "death to war." I never really had the impression that this is what we were in the process of doing . . . We lack goulash and peace.

(He laughs.)

Commandant, yes, sir.

They exit arm in arm. While exiting, together they say:

MAN and **FRIEND** *(together)*: But why do they kill us? Why don't the fascists want us alive? And why us, why don't we want them alive? Why is war everywhere, like tuberculosis? Why have we, we too, against our will, against our intelligence, become bearers of death? Murdered and murderers?

C. The Mountain Bends

In the square.

MAN: At this moment I'm living resistance with such ill humor . . . Fascism has a huge advantage over us . . . These pigs love to make war . . . The more they massacre and destroy, the more they enjoy it . . . Killing? As for us, we can't do it, we are a potency of nature . . . Only nature must be able to make us die . . .

(Pause)

. . . Only nature has the right to cause death . . . But what am I saying? Yes, it's true.

(He looks around, then he looks at the mountain above.)

... An avalanche, a disaster, a mountain's vengeance ...

(He reflects.)

Only nature can cause death. As for us, we are a potency of nature ... An idea is germinating in me, a decision ...

Gunfire and loud noises are heard. Some comrades enter precipitately.

VOICES: Watch out, Man, the enemy is pursuing us, he's almost encircled us, let's retreat.

MAN: Calm down, comrades, I know perfectly well that they are following us. Here's the idea I've had. First of all, retreat. And then, if it's possible despite their strength, double back on your steps and, after I have held them here long enough, take them from the rear. Fight ultimately and only for peace ... Hurry up, the pigs are coming. They are ferocious, so watch out for the women and children. I have figured out how to cover your retreat.

(Pause. He looks around.)

It is possible to make the mountain blow up, just there, above us, we can transform our landscape into a weapon of war ...

VOICES: What is this idea? What are you thinking, what are you suggesting?

MAN: On the mountain there is a big depot of dynamite that was left by the miners. I worked with them. I remember well that they told me of the danger that we had hanging over our heads.

(He laughs.)

Now it's no longer over our heads, but over theirs. We will stop all the fascists and all the pigs who want to destroy us. We will say no to their will to death, we will show them the complicity that ties us to nature . . . and to dynamite. It's not difficult, as for me, I know what to do. And the mountain which has often been our enemy will now be our ally. Retreat, I have to go there now, I am going to make the mountain explode.

(*To the* **FRIEND**, *after all the others have left*)

Shit, you're really lucky to outlive me, I wouldn't bet a dime on it . . . Someone tubercular to the marrow like you, people have to stay away just to avoid catching something . . . And yet . . . Go to it . . . I love you, my old friend . . . Go to it. If all goes well, give my wife a hand.

FRIEND: You are always the same, Man. Always the same rage to live . . . but this time, perhaps you are fooling yourself. In this story, an absurd destiny was introduced into our lives and attacked us treacherously, like a tick . . . I, who am a condemned man, let me serve as a shield for those who retreat with you . . .

MAN: That's it, you have really gone mad. You, the goulash man, generous and heroic? I don't recognize you anymore. Stop. You don't even know where the entrance to the tunnel of explosives is . . . And then you come from the city. Your heart disdains the violence of nature, the glimmerings of its infinite potency. Let me play with the weapons I know.

FRIEND: Let me come with you. Make me feel the decision of a resistant act . . .

MAN: That would just be the explosion of a belly full of goulash . . .

(He laughs.)

In fact, an enormous fart would suffice . . .

(He reflects.)

But that's not the way it happens.

(*He embraces the* **FRIEND** *firmly.*)

Go to it, go quickly, because otherwise I will be obliged to shoot you down right there . . . Farewell, my old friend, lead the men to where they will be able to become guerrilla swarms against the fascists . . . Take care of yourself . . . Tuberculosis is disgusting . . . Did I ever tell you that someday, perhaps, we'll be able to cure it?

(He laughs.)

Farewell, we'll see each other again somewhere else.

The comrades retreat.

COMRADES: Good-bye, Man. You are our defense—and you are also our hope. This mountain has always blocked the light, from now on the village will be brighter.

They go off.

The **MAN** *remains alone.*

MAN *(on the verge of entering the miners' tunnel)*: Here I am . . . What difference is there between bending in order not to break and bending in order to enter the tunnel, becoming a miner once again? Joy of resistance, joy of a sacrifice that must renew the world? What idiocies . . . You simply have to admire the guile of men and this potency of nature that is going to take the enemy's capacity for destruction from behind . . . This would not be possible without someone's desperate rebellion. What a phony part I find myself playing . . . Long live the dead hero! They are right, those who see things this way . . . I've heard such beautiful, empty words about resistance . . .

(He continues to advance, bent double in the tight shaft.)

So much cloying rhetoric destroyed the will to resistance through hollow assertions . . . It's strange: I'll never manage to get back out. Before long I will be blown into the air . . . monster or hero, monster first and hero later . . . What's worth more? In any case, I remain always bent . . . But it's always better than hiding there, before the fascists, and constructing ambushes, and killing as many as possible, even if they are finally not so numerous, one by one, before you kill them. No, this time I've found a good way to bring the mountain down on them.

(He continues to advance bent double.)

It's strange, this love I have for nature, just at the moment when I am on the way to transform it into an act of war . . . In any case, it's best that everything remains so. What will the eagles and the sparrows do when the mountain blows up? Will they feel freer? They will take wing, frightened at first; then nature will seem totally new to them in the midst of the ruins. Fly on, fly on, eagles and sparrows, but come back soon to dwell in the new nature . . .

That's enough! I must hurry.

(He continues to advance bent double.)

The resistance that counts for me is neither killing the enemy nor massacring the fascists—even if it's justified to do so: I haven't done it, but I would be capable of it. No, the true resistance is singular resistance, it's bending in order not to break, it's the rustling of a leaf in the forest, it's permanent sabotage, it's a school of intelligent desertion, an exercise in exodus . . . We must rebel in this world by constructing another, a new one, within it . . . Now I feel like a ferocious beast in the depths of the earth, a beast that is on the verge of winning its battle and yet knows that it will die . . . That doesn't please me, but I must do It . . . I'm not happy to act as a witness, but it must be done . . .

(Thoughtfully)

My love, my sweet, I am sorry, I was so happy with you.

Voices are heard in the distance.

VOICES: *Achtung!*

MAN: She agreed with me that we organize in order to make war on the Nazis and fascists. She was right . . . Regarding this kind of thing, women are almost always right . . . How to stop a river in flood, how to block the ever muddier and more aggressive waves? It's necessary to use a ruse.

(He continues to advance in the shaft, ever more bent.)

She agreed, my wife, that we organize in order to defend life . . . she who had never accepted violence . . . But here, against the Nazis and fascists, it was not our violence at issue, it was theirs. How to act in order to stop a river that is on the verge of drowning us? We must use force . . . better, the ruse to turn nature against death, force against violence . . . A ruse that now puts me to death . . . How much effort . . . Here is the depot at last, here are the fuses . . . My old mining comrades were real professionals . . .

(He looks at the explosive depot and a whole series of machines before him. He is constantly bent double.)

Truly, they left nothing to chance. Good, it's merely a matter of connecting the charges together. To work. I set the detonators. There, the fuse is lit.

(He begins to retrace his steps.)

Am I going to make it out of here bent double? Do I have to begin counting backwards again, like I did in prison, to survive? I'm afraid that I won't make it. This time, I will not manage to conclude the countdown at the other end—three hundred eighty-four . . . three hundred eighty-three . . . three hundred eighty-two . . . Faster . . . I'm not going to make it . . . It's idiotic to die, what can it be . . . I love life so much . . . Two hundred ninety-six . . . two hundred ninety-five . . . And my wife . . . Two hundred ninety . . . two hundred eighty-nine . . . To fight is to force my nature to go against a desire for tranquillity and love . . . Enemy, it's ignoble to give you death, I suffer for having to kill you . . . But it's really not me who is killing you . . . It's the mountain that doesn't want you . . . Two hundred fifty . . . two hundred forty-nine . . . two hundred forty-eight . . . It's nature that's sweeping you away . . . Two hundred thirty . . . two hundred twenty-nine . . . How many times I've climbed these mountains . . . What was beautiful was coming back down, when you got rid of your fatigue with a run: not step by step but in leaps, imagining the hidden crevasses . . . gliding across . . . smooth, mobile, it's what always gave us a boost . . .

Two hundred fifteen . . . two hundred fourteen . . . two hundred thirteen . . .

(He continues to exit bent double.)

I'm not going to make it out of here. Is this how the story of the Bent Man ends? Have they finally enlisted me in their battalions of death? No, no, a hundred times no. I don't want to die . . .

Love is our law, long live freedom and—why not?—long live communism . . . But the disagreeable impression that this time, my ignoble jailers are much too close . . . One hundred seventy-seven . . . one hundred seventy-six . . . one hundred seventy-five . . . Fly, Man, fly. Is it difficult, bent? Straight it's impossible. Do you remember the song that our father sang when he returned from the mine in Belgium? ". . . it's love of humanity!" What imbecility, we are not humanity, we are the life of all and the hope of each . . . One hundred thirty . . . one hundred twenty-nine . . . one hundred twenty-eight . . . Too bad to have to perish . . . Dead in the war . . . Faster, faster . . . Farewell, my love.

The mountain explodes.

ELEGY

Bright light.

WIFE *(pregnant)*: I don't know how to remember the Man, because his flesh belonged to me—he was inside my body, he was my lover, and he became part of me. If remembering is reliving, what can I do now?

Find him again in imagination even though I'm dying from having been separated from him? I can't, he is still in me, he created a child for me that ties me to life . . . He is here . . .

CHORUS: He is everywhere. He brought the mountain down on the enemies. We couldn't believe our eyes. The mountain was transformed into a river in flood, into an avalanche of stones . . . The sky remained blue, and we, we rubbed our eyes when the sunlight stopped being blocked by the mountain that came down and little by little inundated us. Anxiety turned into joy . . . We didn't even hear the cries of the enemy, it was like a giant had smashed it to pieces with one single wave of his hand . . . The new landscape in which we live is the work of that Man who knew how to make Nature a friend . . . Is beauty too a fruit of resistance? That's what is beautiful . . .

FRIEND: When the explosion happened, I ran toward the disaster with my poor lungs, in the mad hope that the Man had survived. Then I saw the last rear guards of the fascists who were fleeing under a shower of debris . . . And in the rumbling that hadn't stopped, they ran with difficulty along the new curves of the valley . . . New hills and totally new little valleys here and there had appeared . . . And along the new courses of unexpected waters that we must now divine, I saw the carcasses of their tanks rolling . . . An earthquake would not have done better . . . And I also felt the Man, monster of revenge or giant of love, who strode laughing through the grotesque ruins of the fascist warriors' ignoble pride. The Man is joyful . . .

CHORUS: Henceforth we live in a great valley separated from the rest of the world, we will no longer need to bend in order not to be broken, and we will all learn to be free.

(*To the* **WIFE**)

We promise you: your child will live free.

(Once again addressing everyone)

And like the legendary Assassins of faraway Persia did, we, from our valley, we will send our best men everywhere to struggle against war. The enemy disaster is for us the leavening of organization. In separation, the swarm makes itself potency. It is potent . . .

WIFE: When the Man bent, night fell. The night has not ended in the ignoble cell of the first days, in the psychiatric hospital, in the tribunal, in the penitentiary . . . There have only been glimmerings, perhaps this was the dawn, when the Man resisted the torture of the experts and the apologists of God and Fatherland . . . But it was a dawn that faded right away, appalled by the cruelty of the times . . . Light was not born the first day of creation but only much later, when men constructed freedom and justice. Comrades, we must learn to struggle in the night, there is no light without war, there is no dawn without destruction and exploitation. I want light for my child . . . My child is certain of light . . .

FRIEND: When this story began, the Man was alone. He was bent, he was truly naked. He trembled with cold and fear. He never justified himself with grandiloquent expressions and assertions of principle: both of those things always end up avenging themselves, they are like the wild swings of a punch-drunk boxer, they blur the sight instead of helping to recognize the adversary . . . On the contrary, the Man knew that solitude, difference, resistance can reveal common behaviors and construct a multitude . . . In this solitude a god lives, a force multiplies . . . On the basis of his suffering, on the basis of our anxiety his strength, like a great wind of life constrained to filter into the fissures of pain, was multiplied so enormously . . . Thus the cataclysm that we all constructed in common could become possible. It is the common . . .

ALL TOGETHER *(addressing the audience)*: This fable that we have told must make us understand that the swarm of the multitude is always capable of creating events of rebellion. A single spark is enough to set the woods on fire! One snowball is enough to provoke an avalanche! Because we live life, each of us is capable of resistance and responsible for the common. We have spoken to you of peace and war, love and rebellion: these are not exotic objects, but the true potency of life. War on war, always, with the soul and the body, singularly and in common. Always. This elegy to the Bent Man in his prison is an elegy to the man who destroys the enemy and affirms hope, a man bent yet again in struggle . . . But always straight, before and after, in the cell as in the mineshaft . . . What we call the Man is nothing other than an affirmation of common freedom . . . Ten, nine, eight, seven, six, five, four, three, two, one.

Blackout.

CITHAERON |

DIDACTICS OF EXODUS
2006

AUTHOR'S NOTE

This play concludes *Trilogy of Resistance*, following *Swarm (Didactics of the Militant)* and *The Bent Man (Didactics of the Rebel)*. Yet, examined closely, this *Cithaeron* concludes nothing. The hope of exodus is swallowed up in tragedy, and its didactics are concentrated on three figures of the human condition: *kairòs* (for Dionysus), *tempestus* (for Agaue), and *typhon* (for Pentheus). Three words that, in different languages and times, express the theoretical decision, the ethical drama, and the political madness that by turns haunt the heart of the one who has chosen exodus.

TRANSLATOR'S NOTE

The text of this play includes many citations from Euripides' *Bacchae*. Antonio Negri draws on the Italian translation by Giulio Guidorizzi: Euripide, *Baccanti* (Venice: Marsilio, 1989). I chose to cite from the English translation by G. S. Kirk: *The Bacchae of Euripides* (Cambridge: Cambridge University Press, 1979). The numbered references to lines of text included in parentheses after each citation of Euripides refer to the latter edition, though the quotations have occasionally been slightly modified to better reflect Negri's choice of terms.

The performance takes place on three levels:
- a small computer screen, isolated in one corner of the stage;
- one or several screens (panels/boards—Web sites) on which the scenes on Cithaeron take place;
- a large screen, which is the square, that is to say, the stage itself.

Music: Schoenberg, *Pierrot Lunaire*

CITHAERON: DIDACTICS OF EXODUS

FIRST VOICE

SECOND VOICE

YOUNG WOMAN

AGAUE

CADMUS

TIRESIAS

PENTHEUS

DIONYSUS

GUARD

FIRST BACCHANT

SECOND BACCHANT

PARODOS

On the proscenium. Distinct figures.

FIRST VOICE: It's a difficult story to tell. In a city convulsed by a crisis, a God intervenes. How can this intervention be represented? We are atheists: recourse to the divine in order to understand the actions and conditions of the human world seems strange to us. Unless it is a matter of events so extraordinary that they remain inexplicable without the intervention of a God?

SECOND VOICE: We are not telling extravagant stories. The responsibility for action and its eventual justification always belongs to us. If we want to speak of the divine, let's state right away that it resides in us. We are thus going to speak of passions that are always found and will always be found exclusively in the consciousness of man. There is no other potency than man.

FIRST VOICE: What happened was extraordinary and terrible. How could we ever understand a mother, Agaue, killing her own son? And how can we show that this wasn't a mad and unjustifiable act but a strong affirmation of freedom?

SECOND VOICE: It's a contemporary story. Of course, *The Bacchae* is an ancient tragedy—but it also speaks of us, of the way in which a world dominated by a tyrant can be revolutionized by the mobile presence of migrants, by the revolt of women against patriarchy, by the desire for freedom of living labor.

(A figure advances to the proscenium and gazes at the audience.)

You are the one of which this fable speaks.

FIRST VOICE: Here is what the ancient story says: "Many are the shapes of things divine; / much the gods achieve beyond expectation; / and what was believed is not accomplished, / whereas for the unexpected, god finds a way. / Such was the result of this story" (1388–1392).

SECOND VOICE: In an unexpected way, thus, because, as you will see, Dionysus, the "god," calls himself "man"—and the miracle is a revolt.

PROLOGUE

A young mixed-race woman is seated at a computer in a computer center.

YOUNG WOMAN *(She reads from the screen the last part of the Parodos of The Bacchae.)*: "The ground flows with milk, flows with wine, flows with bees' nectar. / Like the smoke of Syrian frankincense / the Bacchic god holding high / the fiery flame of the pine torch / streams it from his rod, / with running and dances / rousing the stragglers, / swinging them on with cries of ecstasy / and tossing his luxuriant locks in the air. / Among the joyful cries he makes these words roar out: / 'O onward bacchants, / onward bacchants! / Ornamented with gold of Tmolus' river / to the deep beat of the drums / sing and dance to Dionysus / exalting the god to whom you cry in ecstasy / amid Phrygian cries and incantations / when the holy melodious flute / sounds out its holy uplifting strains, accompanying / you on your way to the mountain, the mountain.' Joyfully / then, as a foal with its grazing mother, / the bacchant springs around with nimble feet" (143–167).

That's magnificent . . . but who are they talking about?

(She types into her computer.)

Ah, there it is . . . "Euripides, *The Bacchae* . . . Cadmus, king, founder of Thebes," good . . . He comes from Asia—he must be dark-skinned, like me—these migrants have always brought elation and the pleasure of life with them . . . "Semele, daughter of Cadmus, mother of Dionysus, impregnated by Zeus, the jealous Hera kills her with a lightning bolt but the fetus Dionysus survives . . . Hidden, he grows up in Zeus' thigh . . . Pentheus, son of Agaue, herself also daughter of Cadmus." Lovely family: Pentheus, therefore, king of Thebes, who wants to preserve order and detests immigrants . . . You could say that he didn't like rebel women either . . . It must be said that these women of Thebes have a character that seems to come straight out of Woodstock . . . Him, on the other hand, he's a real paranoiac. A slightly despotic conservative: "law and order" . . . But what does he want to conserve, what does he want to put in order, since in any case he must take into account the god, who is furthermore his cousin, and who charges into Thebes in order to be acknowledged as an authority contrary to the laws of the city? . . . A god capable of new technologies of life and communication . . . capable of arousing enthusiasm and solidarity never before seen—those that the new knowledges put into practice . . . a demonic god, therefore, one who defies you, Pentheus . . . From the exodus that Cadmus had led Dionysus takes the path again, he reproduces the joy of it. ". . . But if the city of Thebes / seeks in anger and by arms to bring the bacchants from the mountain, / I shall join battle with them at the head of my female furies" (50–52).

The mountain, yes, that's Cithaeron . . . What a strange mountain! Transformed into a community by the women torn from their shuttles and their looms . . . A second nature! Traversed by the flows of communication that render any claim to power chaotic, and that innervate the social relations of desire . . . A forest of trees that is also a network of messages and a storm of passions—but this world, is it not also my own? A computer network open in all directions and constantly renewed in which I live, work, and produce my common? In which I forge a new language capable of conveying know-how and affects toward the common?

Here too there are plenty of bosses who command and who prevent me from fully living this freedom that intelligence and community would nevertheless allow . . . Often my computer is transformed into a shuttle, into a loom . . . If only I could enter this savage and mythical world, this is what I would ask: "Dionysus, help me to escape from this new slavery! Take on human form once again, enter into the community of the network to which I belong, free my potency, free our potency. Beyond all measure! . . ."

"Agaue, mother of Pentheus, kills her son in a Bacchanalian rapture . . ." But Pentheus is a tyrant, a lion who tears to pieces the fawns that roam the slopes of Cithaeron, who wants to control the flows of desire in the network . . . Oh, to what cruel ethics does this world of freedom and potency that is also our own refer? There it is crushed and repressed. Why does my desire need force and my love need violence in order to become free? As for me, I am here, in my suffering and my difficulty, and I invoke a new, potent, and strong Dionysus. I would like to be able to say: Dionysus, gather a new army of maenads and be its head! Here too, in this workplace, in the community that I traverse, and even in this smile that I put on, there is pain—from the difficulty of living oppressed and discriminated against—there is expectation of an extraordinary liberation. How can this savage network in which I am a prisoner be transformed into a free and strong Cithaeron?

I'm struggling like a fawn caught in a snare. Pentheus is always at the head of the dishonest hunters—if I were to free myself from the network, they would loose their dogs against me. Why can't we find a new measure that reverses the relation between those who suffer and those who persecute?!

I don't want vengeance, I want justice. At work and in everyday life, I feel the breath of a new common reality. Illusion or truth? It nourishes the dialogue I have with my comrades, it's a restoring storm. And if the great wind of truth doesn't manage to dissipate the fog of illusion that endlessly imprisons us, oh well, then Agaue, inspired by Dionysus, will come to our aid.

"Well-pleasing in the mountains he, who from the running bands / falls to the ground, wearing / the sacred cloak of fawnskin, hunting / goat-slain blood, the joy of eating raw flesh, speeding / to the mountains of Phrygia, of Lydia, and the / leader is the roarer, euoi!" (134–141).

Damn, I must get back to work, I'll bookmark the sites and return later.

Act I. A

AGAUE, CADMUS, *and* TIRESIAS *meet in the square of Thebes.*

AGAUE (*addressing* CADMUS, *whom she embraces*): My adored Father, how long has it been since our last meeting?

CADMUS: I am always here in Thebes, my daughter, all you have to do is seek me here . . . I live in a retired way, but I am quite present in this city . . . Old, yes, but attentive to what is happening . . . Today, I have come to the square to welcome Tiresias, that old Methuselah. Do you recall him?

AGAUE (*embracing* TIRESIAS): You have found the elixir of immortality? You are the same as twenty years ago, when you supported me in those deathly days when my father passed his scepter to my son. And I, at that time I was already protesting against the dangers that I saw born from that decision.

TIRESIAS: We all knew that Pentheus the hunter was a difficult and scarcely reliable man. Even his father knew it. But monarchical power does not permit vacations. You, Agaue, you did not follow my counsel of seeking peace and compromise. They tell me that you are struggling and that you are plotting for Thebes to find freedom again. You wear the ivy around your head and you dance with young friends, singing hymns in honor of that old, endlessly recurring passion that wants us to be free men in a free world. But, as you know very well, freedom and risk walk in step. Today, extreme limits and sovereign excesses are opposed to civil passions: avoid the danger. I told you this already then, when I urged you to prudence. I am blind, no doubt, but I see a long way . . .

CADMUS: Agaue, my beloved daughter, listen to Tiresias's counsel. If his dead eyes see so far, an old man's gut also knows how to recognize the pain that is foretold. Pentheus thinks that law and order must be the crowning achievement of the constitution of Thebes: the monarch is the one responsible for that. He will never accept your wishes for freedom that reveal symptoms of disobedience, and even less the fact that they are turning into a threat of revolt. He knows that the community today is pervaded by new knowledges and novel possibilities of expression, he will seek to penetrate these flows in order to control them better. So, listen: it's because he recognizes what's new that he is afraid of it. The prudence of a King is also an activity of potent prevention, it's the disarming of the enemy even before he has the strength to act. Pay attention . . .

AGAUE: How unjust are your calls to prudence . . . You, Tiresias, you, father . . . when I was the young mother of a new King, you taught me that I must teach him to interpret and manage the common of our city. That's how you built Thebes, erected its walls, and channeled the savage and differing populations onto a path of Harmony—since that was my mother's name and law. In the city, the unequaled model of freedom, you created conditions so that nature could be continually transformed by labor, so that our sons would be free to run and dance on Cithaeron, and so that they would bring joy back within the walls of Thebes. It's true: today there is undeniable wealth linked to the relations among individuals, and the new technologies of knowledge and communication have made the city even freer than it was. But if this is true, isn't it because there was just this contamination among persons, just this exchange between nature and civil life, that has always seemed to us to constitute the heart of your teaching? At present, Pentheus is cracking down on this order, turning it upside down, destroying it. Why do you reproach me for being what you wanted me to be?

TIRESIAS: My beautiful grown-up doe—this is how my senses perceive your vitality—you know how much the city has changed since then. The wisdom of our legislators is mingled with the labor of the citizens: a new community is born from this cross-breeding, *techne* has transformed the *phusis* in which we planted the bases of the constitution. But the exercise of freedom henceforth no longer goes in this direction, they find the old divinities outmoded and ridiculous, they disobey authority. This new world no longer believes that the legitimacy of the King extends from that of the family, it no longer considers the foreigner as a barbarian, and only through continuous sleight of hand does it respect private property and the rules that perpetuate command and distinction. What has become common in the life of the city prevails over the right to private appropriation; and the new techniques of communication dissolve all hierarchies into equality. We must reflect on this chaotic self-destruction that the exercise of freedom entails . . . Believe me, these are only doubts, but still . . .

AGAUE: Tiresias, how can you imagine that this love that lives in freedom could be satisfied with chaos, and this intelligence that organizes life through communication could derive all its strength from chaos? The problem is different: the problem is Pentheus, because he doesn't know how to adapt to the new *techne* and to the transformations that it entails for our life . . . because he would like to block its creativity. That's what I cannot accept, that's what is driving me to rebellion. Allow me, my fathers, to remind you that Dionysus certainly drives us to transgress, but on the condition that we do so in the world of know-how—and that's why we honor him. Today, like yesterday—and probably tomorrow too—we accuse the god of impiety because he dares incite us to know. The impious thing is the Enlightenment spirit of Dionysus—not his tragic madness but his logical fury, not his enthusiasm but his will to truth. We expect a serene Socratic philosophy from him, an effective *techne*, and the

industrious construction of a second nature. And Cithaeron is there
to embody that project of reason.

CADMUS: You send me back to my younger years, my daughter, you
remind me of that joy that overflowed with common energy at the
moment of the construction of this free city. The mountain, its
open and violent nature, this diversity, this savage desire that other
women, other men, foreigners, barbarians that we didn't call citizens bore within themselves, all that was part of it. And also what
happened later: the constructive integration of *technē* and nature, the
construction of those universal networks that today give shape to our
knowledges—all that made me happy, in the form of a becoming-real
of a vocation that nourished me all along . . . But allow me to insist.
It remains no less true that these reversals must be governed and we
cannot let them follow their own course . . . I do not share Tiresias's
pessimism; but your enthusiasm, rational as it is, leaves me perplexed
and full of doubts.

AGAUE: Then come up onto Cithaeron and let the dances dissolve
your uncertainties. I invite you not to a conspiracy but to a festival of
Dionysus, god of freedom, who is flesh of our flesh, who is my sister's
son, and who was also your favorite godson, oh father, at the moment
when he struggled to be recognized. We recognized him, father, and
if this doesn't quite signify that our body is divine, despite everything
it means that the fact of loving arouses a divine joy in us . . . Come up
onto Cithaeron . . .

TIRESIAS: If I go dance after having wreathed my brow with ivy, they
will say that I am mocking old age! No matter: I will go. It's the joy
of knowing that drives me now and always.

CADMUS: Let us go, Tiresias, I too, even if I am old, I want to banish
the shame of dancing once again for the city. But do not make too
much noise, my daughter!

AGAUE: I will precede you up to Cithaeron in order to prepare for your
coming. The freedom that we adore does not distinguish between the
dancing of the young and that of the old, between black and white,

between man and woman. We live in a language that is common to us, within networks that have been constructed by labor and *technē*, and that serve to develop freedom and not to capture it. But the news of our coming up to the mountain is a message that is already circulating in the serpentine twists and turns of a communication that is truly rid of all chatter. Perhaps it is this, my old friends, that you have not yet understood: this common freedom of ours no longer needs to be constructed, it is enough for it to communicate . . . and today it needs only to be defended against Pentheus. So I am going ahead of you—with the youthful step that new passion has helped me find, my very dear ones . . .

Act I. B

CADMUS *and* **TIRESIAS** *find themselves in the square.* **PENTHEUS** *enters.*

CADMUS: Let us prepare ourselves, Tiresias, hold on to me, I will guide your empty eyes when we climb the mount. Alas, Pentheus is coming . . .

PENTHEUS *(entering the stage racked by great trouble)*: Good day, dear old friends—even if, obviously, one can't really speak of a good day . . . "I chanced to be away from this land, / but hear of the evils that have just broken out in the city— / that our women have abandoned their homes / in fake bacchic revels, and in the deep-shaded / mountains are roaming around, honoring with dances / the new-made god Dionysus, God the son, whoever *he* is; / that wine-bowls are set among the sacred companies / full to the brim, and that one by one the women go crouching / into the wilderness, to serve the pleasure of men— / they profess to be maenads, making sacrifice, / but actually they put Aphrodite before the Bacchic god. / As many as I have caught, with their hands in chains / warders are guarding in the public prisons; / but all who are at large I shall hunt down from the mountain, / Ino and Agaue, the woman who gave me to Echion for a son / and the mother of Actaeon, I mean Autonoë. / I shall fasten them down in iron nets / and put a quick end to this villainous bacchic rite. / It is said that some stranger has arrived, / a wizard and enchanter from the Lydian land, / his hair all fragrant with light-brown tresses, / with ruddy cheeks and the charms of Aphrodite in his eyes, / who daylong and nightlong mingles with young girls / holding out before them his rituals of joy. / But if I catch him within these walls / I shall put a stop to his beating of the thyrsus and tossing / of his locks, by cutting his head clean off from his body. / *That* is the fellow who asserts that Dionysus is a god / and was once sewn in the thigh of Zeus— / the child who in fact was burnt up by the lightning's flame / together with his mother, because she had lied about Zeus being her lover. / Does not this deserve the dreaded noose, / whoever the stranger may be, behaving with pure violence?" (215–247).

TIRESIAS: My sovereign, allow me to enjoin you to be calm and to listen to our counsel.

PENTHEUS: So, what is happening? Even among friends, even among the old, must I find rebellion?

TIRESIAS: This is not rebellion, it is just a cold reflection on the new problems that power must confront. If you will permit it, we will speak.

PENTHEUS: I was taught always to listen to a wise man. But listen, show yourself to be wise!

CADMUS: Do not intimidate our friend, Pentheus, wise counsel addressed to a King is also a reflection of his spirit, if he is not mad.

PENTHEUS: So, let's go, old teeth of Thebes, old dragons of its power, what can you tell me about these new demons that threaten us? Begin, father.

CADMUS: This new demon which you mock, I cannot tell you at what point it will become great for all of Greece. We founded Thebes by appealing to the forces of the earth, to Demeter, to the dry nourishment that allows mankind to reproduce. Here, in the name of Harmony, we have brought together different lineages and constructed the law. That was difficult, we ourselves came from Asia, we wore new clothes; it was difficult to construct an open and productive order. Today, it is precisely on this basis and because of our wisdom that things have changed. Our fellow citizens want to add joy and cooperation, that is to say freedom, to the dry nourishment of Demeter. The wet pulp of the grapes that Dionysus brought us is a gift that integrates life, that helps us to live together and grounds our labor. The more men are linked together, the more they develop techniques and transform the world. Thanks be to Dionysus for this joy and this progress . . . But we must govern it. We must construct a commandment adapted to this new society. The sovereign must use reason to manage this transition, accepting what is inevitable and blocking the dangerous developments . . . You cannot construct dams without also calculating the pressure that the mountain puts on all parts of the basin where the waters are contained . . . If you exclude Dionysus from the project of your government, you risk inciting civil war and arousing destructive passions. These days, I feel a spirit of civil freedom and a demon of revolt that never stop intensifying in the air, both at the same time.

TIRESIAS: ". . . But obey me, Pentheus: / do not imagine that among men, power makes potency; / nor, if you hold an opinion, but your judgment is sick, / take that opinion for good sense. Receive the god into this land / and pour offerings, and be a bacchant, and garland your head. / It is not Dionysus who will force women to be reasonable in love / in the realm of Cypris, but one must watch for this / in their own nature; for even amid bacchic celebrations / the woman who is truly reasonable will not be corrupted" (309–318).

PENTHEUS: I have listened to you with the respect that a young king owes to the founders of the city. What deception! You are not merely old, your thinking too is old and inept. You propose methods of government that are worn through. You tell me to reconstruct a unity, a new culture for the citizens and migrants together, as you did before me. Bravo! But these migrants here are quite different from the ones you were, they don't want to find a land to take them in: they are merely cosmopolitans. They don't debate the wetness or dryness of life, they modify the very notion of it—they propose nomadic, always changing values of knowledge and life. They say of themselves that above all they are men, and, just like everyone else, barbarians and enemies too, they breathe the common air with their mouths and nostrils. They all but consider the division of men into free men and slaves as impious and contrary to nature. They have certainly transformed nature thanks to their labor, but not to the profit of the king and the nation: on the contrary, if they have done it, it's under the illusion of constructing a universal community. The women refuse the rule—that you reaffirmed even in the constitution—according to which the family is the nucleus of power and inheritance the rule of its reproduction. Do you know what they are proclaiming? That they accept and recognize only one single inheritance—the savage inheritance of nomad freedom—and they find the fatigue, dignity, and creativity of life only in this freedom. And they insist: although men think about war and construct a fortress of power in the city, they, the women, are different: their difference is that they want to pursue exodus and drive it toward a different society. What they promise is to have children and to prevent them from serving power. But I tell you with all my authority, the community in which these rebels claim to live and communicate, produce and be free has no principles. For me, it is a community without body, a spirit and a utopia that reek of strangeness. How can I impose order, or even merely discern the material of command, if the subjects shy away from the very conditions of sovereign action? Enough, this must end.

CADMUS: My son, you seem to me beside yourself even when you are reasoning calmly. Imprisoning freedom is always difficult. But when freedom is accompanied by knowledge and youth, it's impossible. I beg you, abandon these extreme judgments. Let yourself be guided by experience, try to reflect, seek to understand before drawing conclusions. It's arduous; but the art of governing, and possibly its guile, consists in that. Seek—or make a pretense of accepting—dialogue, come with us up to Cithaeron. Observe the freedom of these subjects with an eye to dominating them better. Power, deception, and sophistry have always marched in step. Every time the Prince's power seems on the point of wobbling, the gods drive Hermes into the service of Ares.

PENTHEUS: Never. And I despise you, Father, because you give way in the face of the perverse demands of the people and the corrupted sensibility of slaves. A whole world of inferior beings goes up to dance on Cithaeron and raises there a hymn to the destruction of authority. By outraging the eternal essence of the power of Princes, the bacchants claim "to know nothing," and affirm that wisdom and the concept are born of the common agreement of citizens, which transforms nature and strives to create a new nature. They also claim they are immersed in the flows of communication that integrate the knowledges of each and of all, an equal and potent knowledge. I told you that a moment ago: they would like to spread exodus and nomadism. How can you come to agree with this anarchy? How can you support these deliriums of drunkards?

TIRESIAS: Pentheus, you were fathered by a dragon, planted in the viscera of the earth. But today the world is different: life is potent and it resembles instead a serpent that slithers everywhere. It hasn't risen from the depths, it moves agilely on the surface of the earth. I don't know if it's possible to live with this serpent, but—as Cadmus also proposed to you—I know on the other hand that it is perhaps possible to cage it. If you don't know how to risk the joy of new knowledge, then try the risk of government.

PENTHEUS: My anger is growing in the face of the senseless arguments to which these old men are subjecting me. You are completely mad . . . Worse yet: you, who taught me the laws, in reality you are merely atheists. He who honors the god finds him again in the fire that the land generates, and he hates all those who seek to disseminate him and crush him onto the surface of the earth. The serpentine movements of your thought follow the inspiration of Dionysus. It is not free thought, it is licentiousness and vice, it is an unclean mass of serpents that writhes over the land, among the homes, at work; this is not freedom but rebellion. Freedom always lives within the sacred and immutable law of power. I will have to cut off your head, Cadmus; I cannot do that to you, you are the father of this city, that would be insulting the very authority that I am exercising . . . But you, Tiresias, go—before the lowest ranking of my officers severs your pointy head, as we would do with a serpent . . .

TIRESIAS: "Wretched man, how ignorant you are of what you are saying! / Before, you were out of your mind—but now you are delirious. / Let us be on our way, Cadmus, and beseech the god / for this man's sake, savage though he is, / and for the city's too, to do nothing drastic. / But follow me with your ivy staff / and try to support my body, as I will yours. / It is shameful for two old men to fall. Yet so be it, / since we must serve the Bacchic god, the son of Zeus. / Let Pentheus the Painful see that he brings no mourning upon / your house, Cadmus. It is not by prophecy that I say this, / but by the facts—for he who speaks folly is himself a fool" (358–369).

TIRESIAS *and* **CADMUS** *depart.*

Act I. C

PENTHEUS *and* **DIONYSUS**, *who enters the stage as a young man from the suburbs.*

PENTHEUS: This young rebel who excites the women and fools my sovereign fathers, I want to catch him and punish him as only power can, and as my justice knows how to do—I will do it even if he must be called Dionysus!

DIONYSUS *(entering)*: Here I am, I am before you. Good day, King of Thebes.

PENTHEUS: So, you're the one, the mentor of the new liberties against the civil order, the agitator of universality, and the lamb of the women of Thebes! You are not Dionysus!

DIONYSUS: I am a free man.

PENTHEUS: I expected that response. It distorts the truth and it is quite ingenuous. What a mystification. Too bad that Tiresias has departed, it would have been amusing to confront the two of you: him, the timorous old politician, the professional falsifier of reality, and you, who excel in the new art of democratic manipulation of the multitude. So, you are a free man . . . Soon you will be in chains. What could you say to me to justify yourself?

DIONYSUS: That the king does not accept that we "dare to know," that he does not accept civil liberty, and that he transforms the cosmopolitan development of the city, the autonomy of women, and the adventure of common communication into crime. In all these cases, disobedience is divine.

PENTHEUS: Hypocrite! You base your propaganda on what simple people like to believe, you feed them your vicious message of licentious customs and drunkards' euphoria, you celebrate your truth in sectarian mysteries, you proclaim all men equal only in order to dominate them better—not excepting the pain of the life that you sacrifice to your illusions. You are not a wise man, you are a manipulator of consciousnesses, you act horribly, you chain men to an alcoholic lie and women to a licentiousness that defiles them.

DIONYSUS: Pentheus, I didn't come here to destroy you but to convince you. Ever since I first taught men the art of making wine—and my feet still burn from the dance that we improvised together in the vat, the sublime technique that transformed the life, sleep, and imagination of men—since then, therefore, I have never thought that the fact of giving potency to the body and joy to the mind could be transformed into an insult to civil authority and a negation of the gods. Stamping grapes with the feet is only a technical invention. To unite men in imagining a better world is to make audible the symphony of a nature that is not satisfied with itself but, in spite of everything, is convinced of its own potency. Why do you accuse me of perverting the mind even though I have only sought to nourish desire?

PENTHEUS: Because you hide behind these humble, everyday words a will to power that is the reflection of the divine will, and the gods permit this only to kings! With your fables of human omnipotence, you are only helping to introduce drunkards' customs for lost men, and indecent immoderation for those who are tired of the condition that the gods and power have assigned them. You are the cause of disobedience and rebellion. I will punish you. In my city, there is no place for rebel disobedience of the laws, for disorder that threatens the royal measure. The laws were proclaimed in order to reproduce the order of nature. The principle and the commandment are one and the same thing. I will punish you, and you will have to pay the price of your revolutionary madness with your life.

DIONYSUS: Like Cadmus, I too come from Lydia in Asia; like Semele, I have tasted the fire of generation; like thousands and thousands of citizens, I have desired freedom in the fatigue and pain of production. And today, already transformed, I would like to live in a world of free and interdependent communication and cooperation. Whether you want it or not, the conditions for this new life exist, we have constructed them by our labor. Don't disturb the dream that I am living with your threats: it's not only my dream, it's the dream of thousands of men and women. And we are in the process of realizing it. On Cithaeron, our women honor this new nature, beautiful humanity, our land. I am not a specialist in agriculture, but I know that our brothers have made this land a paradise. Demeter herself has abandoned her tragic life as a huntress and feeds there happily. Why can't all these men who know how to get olives and wine, tomatoes and fruit, and so many other exquisite goods from the earth, why can't these men get new orders of the common from their own brains? Bacchus and his wine are a metaphor for all that! Submit, Pentheus, submit to the revolution of the earth and the human brain.

PENTHEUS: You are howling revolt and subversion! Curse you! Why did I let you speak? Like me, along with me, thousands of ears have heard you in secret, lecherously. On Cithaeron, they are already repeating slogans of hatred. Guards, arrest him.

The guards enter the stage.

DIONYSUS: Here are my hands: bind them tight.

PENTHEUS *(to the guards while they bind him)*: ". . . Lock him up close to the horses' / mangers so that he sees nothing but gloomy darkness. / Do your dances there; and these women you have brought with you / as collaborators in evil we shall either sell off, / or I shall stop their hands from this drum-beating din / and own them as household slaves at the looms" (509–514).

DIONYSUS: "I am ready to go; for what must not be, need not / be undergone. Yet payment for these insults / Dionysus shall exact from you, he who you say does not exist; / for in wronging us, it is him that you cast in chains" (515–518).

They all exit.

Act II. A

In the square. A crowd. **AGAUE**, *then* **DIONYSUS**.

VOICES: They've arrested Dionysus. Pentheus had him sent to the Palace prisons. Come on, come on, we must protest. The tyrant intends to assassinate Dionysus, he wants to destroy our freedom. Spread the news to everyone. In the city, in the whole district, in the mountains. Come on, come on, let's free Dionysus.

Voices protesting in the square, in front of the Palace. The agitation grows rapidly. **AGAUE** *appears in the company of a group of men and women.*

AGAUE: Follow me. I know the way that leads to the Palace prisons . . . This door . . . Set it on fire. Be brave, let's open the way to free our friend. Resistance demands action, disobedience is never inactive, power must bend in the face of indignation!

A Molotov is thrown. The door catches fire.

VOICES: "Kindle the bright torch of lightning; / consume, consume Pentheus' Palace!" (594–595).

AGAUE: Let's go, break down the door. Onward! My sisters, my friends, bring the pry bars, break down the barriers. Insert the wedges into the latches, make the locks explode . . .

The door doesn't budge. The fire spreads. Suddenly a sort of explosion is heard, then the earth seems to begin trembling. Explosion or seismic upheaval?

VOICES: "Ah, ah, / quickly will Pentheus' halls be shaken / apart in collapse! / Dionysus pervades these halls: / revere him.—We revere him, O! / —Do you see these stone lintels on the columns / flying asunder? It is the roarer who raises the cry of victory within the building" (586–593).

Are the earth and the heavens allied to help us? Or is this rumbling instead a divine call back to respect for authority? Indignation roused our revolt: has it succeeded in bringing the gods to our side? Nature, in unison with human action, seems to reveal unaccustomed forces. Who can tell us if this unison is our friend? It's only because he acts that man gives meaning to the movements of nature; but when the latter become so impetuous, when the mountain sinks into the valley, when the torrent ruptures its dikes—oh, Dionysus, help us to make nature and rebellion live together!

The rumbling continues until the Palace door ends up breaking into pieces. The demonstrators, knocked to the ground by the explosion, rise. **DIONYSUS** *appears in the midst of the hole.*

DIONYSUS: Rise, men and women of freedom! This is not the time to tremble or reflect, we must continue to spread the revolt. Before long, Pentheus's guards will reorganize and try to silence your voice of justice. The clouds of black smoke are already attracting the forces of repression. These devils are in the process of polishing their clubs, they are donning their armor, they are drawing their weapons from their scabbards, they are ready to kill. Don't you hear the noise of their approaching boots? Let's go, then, we must work quickly, let's organize ourselves to resist. Share the tasks. Let's prevent them from confronting us united. Spread the fire—go, my boy, burn, burn . . . And let's all assemble on the mountain.

VOICES *(responding to him)*: Good, Dionysus, that's what we're going to do . . . Harsh, isolated actions, and we will all gather on the mountain. Good, Dionysus, separate actions against all the symbols of power; attacks and sabotage to impede the possibility of response from the forces of repression. Good, Dionysus, barricades to divide the enemy, in the streets and in the squares. In the suburban alleys, and at last, on the mountain. Good, Dionysus, Luck will help us. The fire and the trembling of the earth have already knocked down the communication lines of power. The enemy is reorganizing, but they don't know where to go. The madness of which they accuse us has become their own. Good, Dionysus, it's the moment to act.

The square empties quickly. Only **DIONYSUS** *and* **AGAUE** *remain, in the glow of the flames that continue to rise across the background.*

DIONYSUS: And so, Agaue, we meet for the first time at the heart of the revolt. A heart that's beating wildly, an untimely leap of reason. . .

AGAUE: I feared for your life, my son, as much as I feared for our freedom. How did you manage to free yourself?

DIONYSUS: It wasn't easy. There were many friends in the dark underground where they took me. When they saw me, they began to protest violently, singing hymns and throwing themselves at the guards . . . The guards left me there and fled, but they locked the doors. Some comrades freed me from my bonds with their teeth and nails. We broke down the doors and set fire to everything that would burn. That's when we heard the rumbling of the revolt coming from outside. The doors of the prison fell under our pressure just as on the other side, in the square, the citizens' rage exploded. We saw Pentheus barricaded inside his apartments, prey to a black rage, asking his slaves to throw water on the flames, then wildly slashing his sword against phantoms of smoke that the fires had raised in the courtyard where he had sought refuge to escape the fire . . . That's where he withdrew to protect himself from the effects of the explosion in the arsenal. Ruin and madness are eating away at him. He falls: we pass before him while he mocks us. The guards withdraw into the few refuges that still exist. They are panic-stricken. They don't manage to repel our attack, they can't communicate with the outside. And that's how the god of freedom ran outside the walls.

AGAUE: The noise of swords and the fracas of weapons can be heard again in there. Let's flee. They are falling prey to fury, they are going to close the city gates.

DIONYSUS: Let me rest here for a moment. I want to make one last attempt to lead Pentheus to reason. You go immediately to where the nearer suburbs of Thebes touch the slopes of Cithaeron. There you will find many immigrants and laborers. If necessary, pass beyond the walls . . . Rouse them against Pentheus's militia and against his old allies, the slaveholding aristocrats. Go, my dear mother, agile and effective . . .

AGAUE *(while exiting)*: "Shall I in night-long dances ever set white / foot in bacchic celebration, hurling / my throat to the dewy air of heaven, / like a fawn playing in the green / pleasures of a meadow, / when it has escaped the terrifying / hunt, beyond the watchers, / over the well-woven nets; / and, shouting, the huntsman / tautens the hounds to their fastest speed? / With straining and with gales of swift / running it bounds over the plain / by the river, rejoicing / in solitude from men and in the shady-leaved forest's saplings. / What is wisdom? Or what fairer / gift from the gods in men's eyes / than to hold the triumphant hand / over the head of one's enemies? / And glory is always sweet" (862–881).

Act II. B

DIONYSUS *on stage.* **PENTHEUS** *enters, accompanied by a guard carrying a computer.*

PENTHEUS *(entering, followed by the guard)*: And in this disaster, the foreigner, the carrier of subversion, has escaped . . . But . . . there he is, before me . . . What are you doing there? How were you able to free yourself? Why are you waiting for me? Do you think perhaps that the law and your condemnation can be corrected?

DIONYSUS: No, when they are just, that's impossible.

PENTHEUS: And so why are you here? If prior to this I had suspicions about you, at present I am certain that you are a troublemaker. You preached Demeter and the joy of the earth before all of us, but you revealed yourself to be a priest of Ares, a carrier of civil war. You have introduced the virus of hatred into the city . . .

DIONYSUS: You cannot call "war" the desire to resist injustice, or this knowledge that revolutionizes techniques, or even the fact that women are affirming their difference within equality. Resistance pervades the human spirit like water pervades the vegetable gardens and nourishes the fruit trees: revolt is its ripest fruit. Look at them: you have never seen them so mirthful and happy, the faces of your subjects who are resisting . . . I'm not the one who must submit to power, you're the one who must bow and bend your arrogance in the face of the rebellion's victory.

PENTHEUS: You're mad.

DIONYSUS: It's the desire for freedom that is mad. It's the love that pervades the bodies that want democracy. Pentheus, henceforth your time is running out. Revolt is always followed by vengeance— because if love has organized a violence capable of redeeming subjects from repression, once this violence emerges from the cave in which it was confined, it continues to work among men. Sometimes it reveals itself, sometimes it conceals itself—but it always ends up reappearing in one way or another, because it doesn't want to return to its cave. Only peace can conclude the adventure. If you want peace, bend before the will of your citizens; if you want to remain king, accept democracy. You accuse me of provoking chaos, but right now the chaos is you. You, not me. Don't you understand that the Palace has collapsed? And that the walls of the city can no longer be defended? All the news that you will hear henceforth from the nearer suburbs and the mountain will seem dangerous to you because it will tell you that the insubordination is spreading. Worse yet: every storm will make you think of revolt, every bolt of lightning will seem a sign of the enemy's victory. When the government is defeated, even nature turns against it. The fact is that here, in the environs of Cithaeron, Demeter found Dionysus. That's why the Bacchic madness opened nature up to the desire of cultures, and *technē* follows desire and interprets it by transforming the earth. Labor constructs community, and in a democracy of labor the difficulty of life is repaid.

PENTHEUS: Your claim to free men from the commands of the sovereign is mad; and your agitation is even more delirious . . . Poor lunatic, befuddled one, fanatic. I would like to be able to keep you in my palace as a monster to show in public, as a buffoon to make the wise men laugh . . . But you have already provoked too many catastrophes, I must kill you . . .

He draws his sword and advances, menacing and furious, toward **DIONYSUS**.

GUARD *(computer in hand)*: My lord, we have reestablished communications. There are many urgent, extremely urgent messages . . .

PENTHEUS *(replacing his sword in its scabbard)*: Tell me, read them to me attentively, even the smallest detail is important in these messages from the police. Tell me calmly . . .

GUARD: "Message number 1. From the suburban command. News of the revolt in the city has reached us. Let us know if it is true, as the rumors say, that the rebels have escaped from prison and set fire to the Palace. Here, we observe numerous comings and goings of strange persons, groups of so-called bacchants and shady individuals. We suspect them of organizing in order to mount subversive actions . . ."

(The **GUARD** *types on the computer keyboard.)*

Pardon, my lord, there is interference, it's not easy to maintain the connection, I can't manage to open the second page. Ah, here it is. "Message number 2. From the intelligence service. Agaue is bustling about frantically in the midst of the rebel groups. She seems to represent their head. When she addresses her companions, she adopts an exotic language: 'Arm yourselves with your thyrsi.' We request permission to arrest her."

PENTHEUS: Mother, what have I done to deserve your betrayal? To provoke your hatred and my despair?

GUARD: Pardon once again, my lord, at this point the interruptions provoked by the rebels are continuous and I am having trouble getting to our information pages. Ah: "Message number 3. From the intelligence service. Having received no response to our request for permission concerning the arrest of Agaue, we are proceeding anyway, given the danger of the situation. We believe that by arresting Agaue, we can perhaps put an end to the expanding revolt. We have assembled a group of agents with the aim of proceeding to arrest her . . ." "Message number 4. We have no news from the group of agents who set out to arrest Agaue. Some scraps of dramatic news have come to us: they have been seized and lynched by the populace."

PENTHEUS: I always saw her shock of flaming hair, but she didn't burn in front of me. Now she is kindling the city.

GUARD: "Message number 5. From the suburban command. We can no longer guarantee control of the territory. All the roads are blocked by barricades. The crops have been set afire. The herds of the big landowners have been slaughtered. It's said that the people in revolt are feeding on living flesh. They have sacked the district's castles, they have killed the aristocrats, they have joined the freed slaves. They have taken the women and children with them."

PENTHEUS *(desperate)*: Heaven help me.

DIONYSUS *(somber)*: The alliance between the heavens and the earth is henceforth achieved . . . So, cry, stupid Pentheus, over your inability . . . How far will the revolt go? Will violence take its vengeance?

GUARD: Pardon, my lord, the network is no longer responding. I'm getting the impression that the rebels have occupied this space too . . . Ah, here it is at last: "Message number 6. From the intelligence service. The news has reached us that certain lords have tried to resist and counterattack the multitude of insurgents with weapons. It's said that they haven't had the chance to use these weapons: flocks of birds, herds of bulls, coiled nests of serpents have fallen upon them whenever they were about to confront the rebels." . . . But what's this? . . . My lord, excuse me, I don't understand, there is another message superimposed on the first, I don't know what it is, you could call it a hymn . . . Should I read it to you?

PENTHEUS: Go ahead, read it.

GUARD: "Let justice go forth manifest, let her go bearing the sword, / butchering through the throat / Echion's ungodly, unlawful, unrighteous, / earth-born offspring" (991–996).

PENTHEUS: That's enough, horrible creatures . . . Phantoms of a past world . . . Abysmal disgrace . . .

DIONYSUS: No, Pentheus, these cruel words are the bearers of happiness, they nourish freedom. You're the one who compelled us to war. We are the future. We are destroying this world that is corrupted by the power that you represent. We are in the process of breaking it into a thousand pieces, little by little, one thing at a time. You wanted a total and unitary system, and that's why it's easier now to dismantle its coherence, dissolve its sovereign line.

GUARD: "Message number 7. From the suburban command. We are on the run. All the villages are in the hands of the slaves and migrants. It appears that the bacchants, with their leader Agaue, are climbing back up Cithaeron: that seems to be the place where the command center of the revolt is set up."

Act II. C

DIONYSUS, PENTHEUS, CADMUS.

DIONYSUS: Your reign is collapsing, Pentheus. Perhaps you have some idea of getting yourself out of it? Those whom you call your gods no longer wish to help you, apparently. It would perhaps be best if you adopted a more docile attitude, a more humble comportment. Would you be disposed to make a deal? Would you be capable of it? You could go up onto Cithaeron with the aim of offering a truce and an amnesty; and in order to discuss the transformation of Thebes' constitution, with the aim of proving the legitimacy of your power . . . Do you believe yourself capable of that? Would you dare to do it?

But I see Cadmus is entering: the old man has not forgotten his responsibility in this whole affair. He is hurrying to join us, he is out of breath. I hope that he will give you good counsel: for a long time he's wanted to go up to Cithaeron. Good day—as if the day that is coming could ever be good—good day, old Cadmus!

CADMUS: I too have gotten wind of what happened in the district, after having directly experienced the hell that was unleashed even here . . . Good day, Dionysus, good day . . . Or rather, good night, Pentheus, my son. What will you do now? My son, I already proposed that you negotiate with the resistance, and by dealing with it, reduce it to a constitutional opposition. But now things have gone too far. I do not know if you will still have an opportunity to present yourself as a statesman: rebellions, when they are profound, deprive negotiations of all legitimacy. Would you be capable, my son, of taking upon yourself the weight of an attempt to go beyond this crisis that your intransigence has provoked and the violence of the insurgents has reinforced? Recall that it is in times of great danger that the true Lord appears . . . The time has come to negotiate and make compromises.

PENTHEUS: I have tried to think of an alternative to merely suppressing the insurrection—but it seems impossible to imagine one. What is at stake? Cadmus, you do not appear to me to be ready to recognize it, any more than your ally Tiresias . . . You speak of reasons of state, prudence, utility, as if all those things were exactly as before and were at stake at this level, but Dionysus and Agaue tell me very clearly on the contrary that it's the authority of the king that's at stake. And your proposals to compromise, which intend to be strategic, don't have even tactical value: they conceal the fact that the bacchants, and with them the migrants and laborers and those who accompany them, have ceased to honor the city's constitution. Suppressing those movements and leading them to discipline would undoubtedly be a quite improbable thing: why seek to modify the appearances of it, weigh down the rhythm of their revolt and purge it of the hope that animates it? Why, therefore, is that a path that must be traveled? What do you want me to do on Cithaeron? When, in the soul of man—not the soul of a *single* man, but that of a large number of individuals—the refusal of order is consolidated, when this refusal has become furious, how can you think that it is possible to bring this subterranean and ferocious, unbounded and proud river into broad daylight in an orderly manner?

(He squirms, somber and troubled. Long, pensive silence.)

If I agree to go up onto Cithaeron, what could I discuss?

DIONYSUS: Excellent question! It is always on the lips of those who believed their power eternal and divine! They know how to speak only of this: the impossibility of power bending to negotiations, the dishonor that follows when power is debated. And they don't know what to do, doubt and uncertainty paralyze them. Enough playing with phantoms, Pentheus. Ask rather if the rebels do not by chance have a different idea of measure and justice and power itself. Yours, transcendent. Theirs: terrestrial, chthonian, democratic.

PENTHEUS: But if it is so, if this savage band of corrupters of the city does not have the same idea of truth as I do, how could I negotiate with them?

DIONYSUS: What do you have to lose in the story? Henceforth, the chips are down . . . Not only in politics, not simply from the point of view of managing the state; no, rather, in the consciousness and lived experience of laborers and citizens. Cithaeron is a young mountain: immense masses of rock are shifting in its breast, they have transformed the valleys, sketching new slopes, configuring a new horizon. Life has gradually occupied the pastures, the frantic activity of the wine growers has replaced the sleepy control of the shepherds—life changes, Pentheus, life gets the upper hand over power. Come up onto Cithaeron . . . And before speaking of the constitution and political movements, come visit a world different from the one that you have known and governed up to the present . . . But you will have to dress differently, you will have to abandon the signs of your kingdom, blend in with nature and the woods. You are curious about the way the maenads behave? You imagine a world of moral corruption and libertinage? In reality, it's merely a question of a new civilization. A new rule that is proposed, an exceeding of the law that constitutes the measure of the time to come.

CADMUS: I do not know if Dionysus is right. But in order to command, above all it is necessary to know; in order to crack down, above all it is necessary to experience crime; in order to win, it is necessary to evaluate the enemy's forces. Let's go, Pentheus, throw yourself into the adventure. A sovereign is not simply the guardian of the law . . . He is not only that.

PENTHEUS: Good—I will go see what is happening up there, I will go to inform myself. If the problem had not been presented to me in this extreme, insurrectional form, perhaps it would have been possible to reach agreement by means of intermediaries. But what seems to be at stake here is the very function of sovereignty—a priest would say that divinity is put in question, because men suddenly have a new way of thinking that makes the gods useless and dangerous. Good, I will go see what is happening up there: but how to do it?

DIONYSUS: How? Won't you admit to yourself that the simple fact of posing the question means that in reality you consider the thing impossible? Here's how: you will have to abandon your royal vestments—the king will have to show himself naked. Just as Agaue did before you, you will have to enter into the game and imagine that you are the multitude, you will thus have to take on an aspect of it. You must be flushed crimson with the passion of the common and the love of otherness. No, that's impossible for you! You don't have the strength to become different, you will not know how to interpret the supple line that traces the radical thought of the transformation of the world. The duplicity of sovereign reason will always reveal you as a hypocrite, no one will believe it. So, get undressed, I defy you to do it!

PENTHEUS: I will never do it. Unlike you, I don't have the duplicity of the hermaphrodite. Your own problem is not undressing yourself but adorning yourself in increasingly artificial and appealing ways . . . You are a decoy.

DIONYSUS: I am proud of my capacity to be at once inside and outside of things, over and under, in the relations of the flesh as well as in the rational language that constructs civil life. In the old days, when one was plunged into myth, it was rare that one managed to get out. Today, critique and the rational gaze on the world can, on the contrary, be developed from the outside. Thus is the mystery of power unveiled and the project of democracy clarified. There you have my duplicity, Pentheus: hermaphrodite, yes, but one of sense and knowledge, critical know-how and democratic hope: that is what I oppose to you.

CADMUS: Calm down, my children. This is not the time to compare your conceptions of life and power. What is necessary is to find a reasonable solution to a state of civil war.

PENTHEUS: Quite so. I will take no notice of Dionysus's provocations and I will put on the clothes of a peasant—or those of a rebel from Cithaeron—in order to understand what is happening up there and decide what to do.

DIONYSUS: I find your decision wise. But when you confront the insurgents, will you know how to imagine another decision—a decision different from the one that now and always haunts your heart, and that I consider malevolent?

(To himself and in a low voice)

Things have gone too far, the basin of passions has overflowed—I have the impression that the water held back by the glaciers and dikes of the mountain is ready to hurtle down all at once: nothing will be able to stop the flows, a chasm has opened up . . . In your heart, Pentheus, the will to be sovereign and the impossibility of modifying your government confront one another with too much ingenuousness.

In the old days, Ulysses practiced all the arts of sovereign trickery, but only his dog saved him from a deadly defeat. Here, there won't even be a single dog inclined to help you.

(*To* **PENTHEUS**, *in a loud voice*)

So, prepare yourself, Pentheus—if even Cadmus is dressed as a bacchant, it will be necessary that you too do likewise if you want to understand what is happening.

PENTHEUS: Never. I will disguise myself not as a bacchant but as a peasant.

DIONYSUS: Let's go. Pentheus, set out for the mountain.

PENTHEUS *and* **DIONYSUS** *exit.*

Act III. A

Only a corner of the stage is lit: the computer service already seen in the prologue. The **YOUNG WOMAN** *is in front of a computer. For a little while, she works, then she stops.*

YOUNG WOMAN: A little rest at last . . . A break . . . I can return to that story I found this morning.

(She taps at the keyboard.)

There is it, the King of Thebes' site. Look at that, Pentheus is walking in the company of Dionysus. What could have happened since this morning? Ah! They're going toward Cithaeron! He is disguised as a peasant, Dionysus at his side. The site allows me to follow them directly. Let's see . . . They're debating . . . I can't manage to get the sound. Ah, yes!

Across the big screen: light on the whole stage. Banner: KING OF THEBES SITE.

PENTHEUS: The climb is rough, these clothes that I'm wearing weigh too much . . .

DIONYSUS: Yet the robes of power were heavier still . . . But it is true that there is a horrible heat wave on the mountain today, a suffocating heat that takes you by the throat, impossible to escape it . . . Are you sure you want to keep climbing? Do you really know what you want? Do you really hope to redefine your power on the basis of the relationship that you are going to establish with the women of Mount Cithaeron?

PENTHEUS: I will observe them. I will spy on them. Perhaps that will allow me to understand what the eventual lines of a new exercise of sovereignty are. It's not really that I believe it . . . But the situation is exceptional, I must bend myself to the exception in order for power to dominate it and perhaps turn it back, in order to take back in hand the full exercise of power. Sometimes everything has to change in order for nothing to change . . .

DIONYSUS: Let's go, keep walking slowly and with perseverance. Are you sure you want to continue? The trees are listening to us and your most secret aims are known. We are inside a kind of magical resonance, and I don't really know if the fact of being heard as we are will earn us sympathy or hatred. I didn't agree to accompany you up onto the mountain in order to be your guarantor. My goal is only to make you aware that, in the game of sovereignty, a king is always subject to his subjects. And the will of the citizens, which is sometimes capricious, can be just as cruel . . . all the more so, undoubtedly, since royal power itself has been capricious and cruel . . . And then when a king changes clothes, it's a bit like he was naked . . .

The connection is broken. The **YOUNG WOMAN** *taps at her keyboard, irritated. The light shrinks down to the computer service.*

YOUNG WOMAN: The image is gone. Ah, another site address, what could that be? Agaue's site. Let's try it, you never know.

Banner: AGAUE SITE.

FIRST BACCHANT: Agaue, they have seen Pentheus climbing Cithaeron. They say the king is naked.

AGAUE: A naked king is a scandal and cannot command.

SECOND BACCHANT: He appears to be wearing women's clothes . . .

FIRST BACCHANT: That's not true, he's behaving like a spy and he's dressed like a peasant. Dionysus accompanies him.

AGAUE: Keep an eye on him and try to determine his path. And don't forget: if Dionysus accompanies him, it's because he wants to deliver him to us after having made him believe that there was a possibility of negotiating . . . Watch out, be careful, keep me informed. We must take him alive—but if he flees or uses stratagems, kill him.

The image becomes blurry. It freezes. The light shrinks again to the computer service. The **YOUNG WOMAN** *continues to tap on the keyboard.*

YOUNG WOMAN: How can a mother give the order to kill her son? There's a link to another site.

Banner: DIONYSUS SITE. Return to the whole stage.

DIONYSUS: People of Cithaeron, bacchants and men, serpents, lions, and bulls of the mountain, here is the tyrant disguised as a peasant, here is the spy. The tyrant still hopes to be able to preserve his power by reaching an agreement with you. His courage is equal to his guile, but alas, among the things of the world and faced with truth, shrewdness is quite a miserable thing. Cynicism is stupid. I am going to deliver him to you, strike him down. He is trying to act like a child—but children are more malevolent than the elderly. It's not that he is dressed as a peasant, no, it's that he's naked: the King is naked. He has lost all the symbols of his sovereignty during the ignoble exercise of his power. Abandon all respect for the sovereign, he doesn't deserve it. Abandon all feelings of vengeance, act with justice. He has expressed a fury that insults the law—strike him down with the same fury.

Abrupt change of site; the image jumps and changes. Banner: AGAUE SITE.

AGAUE: I am asked how a mother can give the order to kill her own son. They insist: nature, morality, and history forbid, condemn, and reject this repulsive crime: *ab aeterno!* Hypocrites! I could answer that I, Agaue, am queen—and that, just like my son, I participate in that majesty through which the originary violence of power is incarnated. That is what gives me the right of legitimate death. I could also answer that I am a woman: why do I not possess the patriarchal prerogative of the power of putting to death? How much fear and infamy do we find in the definition that man has attributed to woman, making her the only creature among all females to enjoy the power of giving birth to the exclusion of all else? But with all that, I have not yet answered the question. The more I turn it over in my head, the more the pity that has always animated my life and the love that has always nourished my existence are transformed into a terrible pain, into a desperate scream that rises from my entrails and refuses any justification. There are seven knives embedded in the heart of a mother who wants to kill her child; but how many are there in the heart of an infanticidal mother? Nevertheless, here, in the heat that envelopes the mountain and makes the earth ooze with violence, here I recognize myself in a totally different drama—the recognition of justice denied and the desire to reestablish the city are transformed into war. I have drawn the saber, the sword of the just. Don't ask me anymore why I must go kill my own son. Dionysus guides me—god is serenely being made man. Dionysus himself would not know how to answer this question. Why are we compelled to war by love? Why do we tremble at necessity?

BACCHANTS: "Appear as a bull or a many-headed / snake or a fire-blazing lion to behold! / Go, O Bacchus—around the hunter of bacchants, / with smiling face cast your noose; / under the deadly herd of maenads let him fall!" (1018–1022).

Act III. B

YOUNG WOMAN, DIONYSUS, AGAUE. *The scene opens on the computer service.*

YOUNG WOMAN *(still tapping on the keyboard)*: Here it is, I'm there.

Banner: DIONYSUS SITE.

BACCHANTS: "Let us dance to the Bacchic god, / let us shout aloud the disaster / of the dragon's descendent, Pentheus; / who took female raiment / and the fennel-rod, Hades' pledge, / in its thyrsus-shape / with a bull to lead him into disaster. / Cadmeian bacchants, / you have made your victory song a famous one— / to end in wailing, in tears! / A fine contest, to embrace your child / with a hand dripping with blood!" (1153–1164).

YOUNG WOMAN *(overwhelmed)*: My God, what is happening?

The space of the computer service and the space of the sites come together and become confused. **DIONYSUS** *appears beside the* **YOUNG WOMAN.**

DIONYSUS: What is happening? There are so many things happening, like every time a revolutionary fervor succeeds in setting the earth on fire. Much later, they made this story—which was certainly not a garden party but which had a meaning, and whose cruelty was the bearer of freedom—they made this story, therefore, into a terrible fable. Just a cruel fable. They wanted to read into this fable feelings of guilt instead of the joy of an experiment. A mother killed her son! No! A mother killed a tyrant! The severed head that this mother brings into the city on the end of a pike is the head of the Lion of Libya, the head of the monster that persecuted us. Agaue is Saint George, Agaue is justice, Agaue is a star. This story is no different than what the biblical story tells us when it exalts Judith triumphantly carrying the head of her lover, him too an enemy and tyrant justly put to death. What we must understand and recount is not how resistance is transformed into violence, but why. Yes, it's true, I led Pentheus up Cithaeron and I exposed him to the view of the bacchants in revolt. I warned them that Pentheus was spying on them lustfully from high in a tree. His mad hatred of freedom and his fanatical sense of power compelled him to consider every spontaneous and joyful act as immoral and illicit; his conception of the world was mixed with suspicion, his only religion was henceforth made up of manias and superstitions. When I led him to the mountain—since he had been compelled to negotiate by a constantly widening revolt— I tried to convince him that he did not have to gamble on reticence and guile if he wanted to open the discussion. Yet the further we ascended, the more everything happened as if he had become a savage beast once again; he began to sniff out the area like a ferocious hunter, he bestowed aggressive epithets on his possible interlocutors, he ceaselessly repeated the refrains of warrior songs and wanted them taken to heart . . . Poor man, poor imbecile—as the majority of individuals to whom the hereditary line or distinction has granted power so often are . . . But what a dangerous and infamous man too in his behavior, sometimes opportunistic as well, and aggressive, and domineering . . . We see him as a lion, but doubtless he was only a hyena. The man must, despite everything, preserve a little charisma once divested of his royal finery and the symbols of his potency, if he really wants to represent power . . . But Pentheus was nothing but unworthy, he cried like a child when he was surprised by the sword—he was naked, but he hadn't understood that what he offered to view was neither ingenuousness nor poverty. He said only unworthy things, he did only unworthy things. What took place thereafter didn't even resemble a great act of regicide . . . Pentheus was the only one responsible for this misery . . . Little by little, however, when the news had spread among those who, in the mountains, were gathered at Agaue's call, the climate abruptly changed. The terror undergone, the fear fed by clandestinity, the lacerating decision to resist authority, all that suffering was let go, joy got the upper hand over resentment and dissolved the sad passions that haunted the revolt; and the impression of having done a just thing was generalized—because the regicidal act was ultimately seen for what it was: the love of freedom against tyranny. But I see Agaue is coming . . .

AGAUE (*entering and approaching* **DIONYSUS**): I heard your reconstruction of the facts, Dionysus. And I agree with you. Nevertheless, let me add a few words—because execrations are now beginning to take shape everywhere against the crime of a mother. What happened was neither a regicide nor a tyrannicide, but an infanticide committed under the influence of alcohol. It was not from drunkenness but from passion; and it was not Bacchus who excited my spirit, but love. My hands are stained with a son's blood, it is true; but this abandonment to common madness that drove me to hate the tyrant, is it not more worthy than the mute pain to which a mother is constrained when the tyrant decides to kill her children or send them to war? What meaning could maternal pity still have? When the pity of mothers is publicly recognized only because it involves crying for all the grief that power imposes on us . . . And what meaning can it have to dismiss the tyrant's madness and the indignation—and even the fury—that, on the other hand, is constructing the desire for freedom without deciding between them? I lived at the center of this tragedy—at the same time the mother of the tyrant and the one responsible for the revolt—and I suffered in the harshest way of all. Perhaps you think that it is easy to separate the blond curls of your own child from those of all the little boys who were the children of victims persecuted by the tyrant? This anxiety lasts so long that one becomes incapable of affirming that love is the potency of extracting oneself from force—and that the madness of the democratic revolt is really an expression of love . . . The drama is not over in my conscience; the good gods and the bad gods are almost completely mixed up from now on; and the more distance that is established, the deeper the pain becomes, and the more terrible and atrocious this act seems to me . . . There is nothing heroic in putting a son to death; and this violence which was necessary to my life is in the process of transforming itself into despair . . . God forgive me—God will not forgive me.

DIONYSUS: Of course: no god can forgive you—because no god exists who is outside our passions. These passions we attribute to them. This is how we constructed an Olympus of impious deities, from whose protection Pentheus thought he could benefit . . . I too am considered a god—the passions that I promote are those that destroy all divinity: love, knowledge, the common. The joy of living: that, then, is the demon that drives us on and never abandons us. I am a stranger in my own country and always on the run, I am a woman, I am Socrates drinking the hemlock for the love of truth . . . What do you want a god to be, if not this desire for freedom that is inside every one of us?

He exits.

Act III. C

In the square. Funeral pyres are glowing everywhere. Crowd. **CADMUS** *and* **AGAUE**.

CADMUS *(entering)*: The lands of the city and the district are covered with corpses. The madness of power and the rage of those in revolt have plunged us into a swamp of pain on whose surface float the bodies of the mutilated and the dead. The fog rising from this lagoon is a death shroud. The birds that lived in these marshes had lively colors; they have turned gray. The litanies of grief are intermingled with howls of despair. Deep inside each one recognizes all the immense pain of the city. Ah, if I were not king again today, after the death of my son, I could occupy myself with nothing more than his body, reassembling the horribly scattered pieces that I have gathered one by one in rage and pity . . . But the unhappiness of the city strikes me full in the face. I can't manage to think of a single grief when thinking of thousands of others would be necessary. And still now, I ask myself how the conflict became a war, why the political struggle was transformed into carnage where brothers attacked brothers . . . When I built my power upon Thebes, the whole city lived through Thebes: it was a city of brothers. Poverty transformed the citizens into brothers . . . How were the passions of the citizens able to become violent, how was the love of freedom able to make itself into an assassin? Each piece of Pentheus, each piece of this dismembered body seems to be a piece torn from the city. To reassemble a body . . . ah, what a terrible task that represents . . . What an atrocious tragedy we have experienced . . . What is the trouble worth? Pentheus was a tyrant. But the wisdom of the ancients—which holds an infinite potency— tells us that even the tyrant is a king, that he is the unity of the social body. Why, by dint of wanting to transform the constitution, did we end up tearing his flesh to pieces like birds of death? Why does freedom need terror? I am crying for my son, I am crying for this absurdity, this violence. I despair for man and for his fate . . .

(*He notices* **AGAUE**.)

Agaue, my daughter! Unhappy mother, answer my doubts, resolve my problems: tell me why love puts to death, why freedom undoes every limit, every measure of social construction! Tell me of the deepest grief and pain that have wounded you . . . Tell me also with that extreme hope that drove your thought and supported your act.

AGAUE: Console yourself, father, your grief is no less than mine, your royal preoccupations are no less important than mine. On the contrary: the wrenching that Pentheus imposed on my belly when he was born, and which transformed my pain into joy, is turned upside down today and instead unleashes its violence over me. My belly groans now with pain as much as it trembled with joy at giving life. And for me too, the grief is redoubled by the city's disaster. But, dear father, you should not attribute the fault to the boundlessness of the desire for freedom, you should not transform this horrible story by falsely reading its origin in the paradoxical interweaving of freedom and terror. No. The city's pain was longer and stronger than what we experience today, after what seems to you an unexpected revolt. I, on the contrary, I expected it—because the accumulated pain was immense and pervaded all the nerves of the city. I don't want to remind you now of how—and with what fury—Pentheus tightened the stitches of your old constitution which had formerly integrated the migrants, which had given women a role in public life, which had pushed for cooperation in labor and incited a sustained transformation of nature. It was not only the blockage of this experience of citizenship that provoked the insurrection—but also the feeling of infinite pain that each body had to pass through and submit to every day, at a time that had suppressed hope. There you have the causes of the revolt. Before his body was torn apart, Pentheus himself had torn apart the union of power—and each one had to undergo the effect in the singularity of his pain. Pain always lacks ideality, it can go beyond measure and express itself beyond the limit. The demand for freedom is rooted in this obscure and potent foundation: it is a refusal of pain. Don't cry for the consequences that this entails, O my father, no, cry for the causes that are at its origin. Quantitatively, the terror that the insurgents could produce is infinitely smaller that the pain that they endured. And me, I continue nevertheless to cry for my son, assassinated by terror . . . What terror do I speak of? That of my fellow citizens, or that which Pentheus turned against himself? Boundlessness does not fit into the paradoxical relation that is established between freedom and terror. Boundlessness is when pain can no longer be contained. Once pain has surpassed all measure, vengeance, which we have nevertheless excluded from the order of private rights, reappears despite everything as a thirst for justice . . . Beyond imagination, beyond measure . . . See, father, I don't understand how you, who were the first legislator of this city, who instituted a constitution of peace in Thebes in order to respond to the migrants' fatigue, to the women's suffering, and to the exploitation of laborers—I don't understand how you could feign not understanding that it was justifiably on the basis of this burning mixture of freedom and terror, pain and chaos that you set your constituent power to work. What we experienced anew during the revolt is the same mystery that guided your untimely decision then. What is to be done now, amid these ruins? Will we have the capacity to press the freedom we have reconquered and the common respect that we have for one another on to the reconstruction of the city? I cry for our defeat, Cadmus, this defeat that we, the founders of Thebes, have undergone through the horrible end of Pentheus. And then, at the moment when we are busy around the pyres in pain, difficulty, and grief, a wind of freedom comes to our aid. Perhaps in extremity democracy is possible.

EXODUS

Return to the computer service. The **YOUNG WOMAN**. *Gradually, the light widens: we slowly discover the square. The* **YOUNG WOMAN** *and* **TIRESIAS**.

YOUNG WOMAN: I've listened to them attentively, all these debates that they have held. I can't manage to understand the stakes—but every time that a problem rises back to the surface, I recognize it as belonging to me. My problems as a mixed-race and precariously employed woman . . . I would really like to speak with those actors about them. But they come and they go, they pass rapidly across the screen, they cross the backdrop, they are absorbed by the tragedy they are living to the point that it's vain to try and isolate them in order to establish contact with them. They stream by. They are matter in movement, flow that is impossible to channel, flexible and rapid. Stop, movement! Let's stop it—let's construct a body that can explain movement . . . But perhaps it's too late . . . Tiresias is approaching . . .

(Bright light on the whole stage.)

Perhaps I am going to get to discuss it . . . Tiresias, good day . . .

TIRESIAS: Good day, good night, leave me in peace . . . I am going into exile. I who am blind, I am blazing the trail for those who can see. That's what always happens in eras of transition, when imagination alone allows us to advance on a path made of void.

YOUNG WOMAN: Where are you going? Where do you intend to lead your company?

TIRESIAS: And who knows that? It's not the goal of the path that's fascinating, it's the movement. It's not an ideal hidden at the very end of the course that pulls us forward, it's the potency that we have constructed in ourselves. That's what drives us.

YOUNG WOMAN: Careful, Tiresias, from now on the danger is great.

TIRESIAS: The risk that awaits us is not a problem for me. We have no god who guides us, just some small glimmers behind us. I am heading toward a cosmopolitan community, toward a world where women and men are equal, where brothers who labor love one another and love the world. The last grief that we celebrate is that of Dionysus: he presented himself as a god, we have sent him back as a man. Nevertheless, even if we are unhappy, we are still believers. Will there ever be one single man to make himself a god and allow us to construct some joy and freedom?

YOUNG WOMAN: Go on, Tiresias, I will accompany you as far as I possibly can.

AFTERWORD |

Staging the Plays
BARBARA NICOLIER

Toni Negri's *Trilogie de la différence* gave rise to two fully staged versions at the Théâtre National de la Colline in Paris, but two of these three plays were previously premiered on their own, under my direction.

The premiere of *Swarm* took place at the Théâtre de Vidy-Lausanne—Espace Théâtral Européen, Switzerland, in June 2004, with Évelyne Didi cast in the role of the Man. With the composer Gabriel Scotti, we worked out a sonic space that allowed the actress to produce live the lines of the Chorus, with her voice amplified and increased, while dialoguing with her natural voice when she was speaking the lines of the Man. A year later, simultaneously with the transfer of this production to la Colline's small stage, I directed *Swarm* on the big stage in a joint production with University of Paris I–Sorbonne. Sixty-nine student interpreters took on the words of the Man and the Chorus randomly and sometimes simultaneously, live and in several languages. The University of Paris I–Panthéon/Sorbonne and the Théâtre National de la Colline established a partnership in 1997 through which more than five hundred students interpret and sometimes premiere plays by such writers as Dorst, Enzensberger, Vinaver, Müller, Brecht, Bond, and Masséra; after our production of Negri's *Swarm* in June 2005, we premiered *Cithaeron,* in the same framework and more skillfully, in June 2007.

The first production of the complete *Trilogie de la différence* took place in October 2007 at la Colline with French public radio station

France Culture as the main producer for subsequent broadcast of what was, at that time, Negri's complete theatrical works. We used the time (ten days of rehearsals for three actors: Évelyne Didi, Gilles David, and Pierre-Félix Gravière) and specific technical conditions to create a unique set for performance that highlighted the epic aspects of this dramatic writing and allowed the actors battling with the text and the making of the sound, its projection, mixing, and recording to be seen together and live. We decided to place the whole technical staff in the middle of this huge, eighteen-meter stage as the three actors sat on high stools downstage for the first two plays and upstage for the last, addressing their text over lecterns to the real protagonists, the audiences who sat in the theater.

The choices for the Chorus changed according to each play's needs. In *Swarm*, the actress playing the Man answered not only to the other two actors assuming the role of the Chorus and deciding themselves randomly in each instant to speak such or such a line, but also to fragments previously recorded by the author. For sequence D1 a constellation of sounds stood for a multitude: we projected voices of children from the Radio France choir school so that the rustling of the possible surrounded the actors and audiences. For *The Bent Man*, the actors portraying the three main characters (Man, Wife, Friend) had to answer to the recorded voices of the Policemen, the Doctor, the Priest, and others, which had been caught outdoors in an almost natural environment. We took care to localize the projection of these voices, so they came to the audiences slightly altered from a small loudspeaker above them. For the terrible transition—the final sequence C where "the mountain bends"—instead of the noise of an explosion we heard the bodies of executed partisans dropped into the waters of the Venice lagoon at the end of Rosellini's film *Paisa*. We took the opportunity in "Elegy" to invite other voices (among them the author and his translator) to meld in the projection with those of the actors live on stage.

For *Cithaeron*, the actors sat upstage as the technicians worked at their desks downstage as if it were the platform, and the technician who played the Young Woman took care of the titles and stage directions from the first play onward. Her situation made her the central figure of the whole set. The two spaces were distinguished by lights, which also allowed them to exist simultaneously.

Agaue, Pentheus, and Dionysus spoke to the recorded voices of two great directors in contemporary French theater: Alain Françon as Cadmus and Jean-François Peyret as Tiresias. The part of the bacchants was taken by the voices of friends projected from the same spot as the multitude in *Swarm*. For "Exodus," with the stage emptied of actors and technicians, the Young Woman reached Dionysus's site only by speaking with the vocal presence Tiresias.

The second stage version of the trilogy took place in June 2009, in the same partnership with the Sorbonne. It involved a long period of work (two rehearsals a week from November to June) and a great number of student volunteers as actors, most of whom were innocent of any theatrical experience. The first academic term was dedicated to sequence A in *Swarm* (Indignation/Hatred/Temptation), following modes invented for each rehearsal according to the texture of the text, which prompted us to adjust our speech to the very letter of the text.

We began by setting up two readers as the Man and the Chorus, as a *basso continuo* that worked as a fulcrum for the seventy other actors, allowing them to take hold of such or such a fragment on the spot. Then each actor took care to address his part to a precise and localized listener in the audience. Each actor was thus put in a position of being responsible for his own words and could elaborate his own conduct during the rehearsals, which after much practice allowed the actors to shift skillfully from "I" to "we." We kept rehearsing these opening scenes during the entire elaboration of *Trilogie de la différence*, and then the whole play until they took on their true status of expository scenes. We then proceeded to the distribution of the text into several "conductors" *(conduites)*. These fragments were drawn by lots by the actors and set as they were, following the chronology and morphology of the scenes. Thus each actor became independent from his predecessors and his followers, assuming his part in the present and grasping the text bodily. This interdependence granted free movement to the patterns working inside the writing, so that the actors became acute enough to knowingly exchange their parts. We built the sequences by experiencing the strangeness of this dramatic language that we took amusement in distancing from ourselves—for instance, dissociating the subject from the verb. We also took license to speak simultaneously the pivotal terms that span the three plays—terms that increased in forthrightness and precision at each rehearsal.

Because the actors were many and had acquired great skill thanks to their work, we could divide the parts without damaging the understanding of the plot and its stakes—quite the reverse. Thus established, this plural speech allowed us to work on the signs and *gestus*, helping to identify the "characters" or the courses. Watchful of the distinction, the poses of power and the effectiveness of potency were revealed with the help of a few elements that were made into signs throughout the three plays: material signs (such as the red cloth in *Swarm* becoming the scarf on the Friend's neck in *The Bent Man* and ending up adorning the hair, wrists, and ankles of the actors playing Dionysus in *Cithaeron*), but also poses and the occupation of space like so many signs of difference. When the text and the stage directions were understood by all, the actors could have a go at the opposite part before they chose and took a stand. We also called on the skills of students in various fields; for instance, the actors who knew music worked during the year on the musical indications within the plays and integrated the required Schoenberg pieces into the performance.

Our two performances took place after a particularly rich year, which included an occupation of the Sorbonne, active strikes, and demonstrations of research workers supported by, and sometimes associated with, many students. The second performance was the best: in two hours and ten minutes of experiencing each other and respecting the text to the letter, the actors gained freedom, virtuosity, and autonomy.

Translated by David Tuaillon

TRANSLATOR'S NOTES |

Translator's Introduction

I thank Dan Cottom for his cogent advice on my Preface; Michael Hardt for his careful reading of my drafts and his unfailingly useful suggestions for improving them; Barbara Nicolier for access to documentary materials related to her productions; and Toni Negri for his constant encouragement during the translation of these plays.

1. Michael Hardt and Antonio Negri, *Multitude: War and Democracy in the Age of Empire* (New York: Penguin, 2004), 189.

2. Ibid., 150.

3. Ibid., 221.

4. See Timothy S. Murphy, "To Have Done with Postmodernism: A Plea (or Provocation) for Globalization Studies," in R. M. Berry and Jeffrey di Leo, eds., *Fiction's Present: Situating Contemporary Narrative Innovation* (Albany: State University of New York Press, 2008), 29–45.

5. Gilles Deleuze and Félix Guattari, *A Thousand Plateaus: Capitalism and Schizophrenia,* trans. Brian Massumi (Minneapolis: University of Minnesota Press, 1987), 12.

6. See Joseph Tabbi, "American World-Fiction in the Long Durée," in Berry and di Leo, *Fiction's Present,* 73–100, and especially William Smith Wilson, "Michael Hardt and Antonio Negri: Irreducible Innovation" (2005) in *ebr: electronic book review* at http://www.electronicbookreview. com/thread/endconstruction/lateral. Wilson writes: "Their books are self-exemplifying, and as such stand as autonomous poetic structures. They write from within, and in behalf of, a world-design that is radically different from the world-designs of most of their critics. Their materialist world-design

should be thought of as their world-poem, surely reflecting their life-poems, yet not the tragedy but the comedy, *La Vita Nuova.*"

7. Bertolt Brecht, "On the Theory of the *Lehrstück,*" cited in Jonathan Kalb, *The Theatre of Heiner Müller* (Cambridge: Cambridge University Press, 1998), 26.

8. Fredric Jameson, *Brecht and Method* (New York: Verso, 1998), 63–64. Jameson's preferred example is the linked pair of plays *Der Ja-sager* and *Der Nein-sager* (*He Who Says Yes* and *He Who Says No*), which stage different resolutions to the same conflict.

9. Karl Marx, *The Eighteenth Brumaire of Louis Bonaparte,* in *Surveys from Exile,* trans. David Fernbach (New York: Penguin, 1973), 146.

10. Jameson, *Brecht and Method,* 64.

11. Hardt and Negri, *Multitude,* 201.

12. Ibid., 199–200.

13. Ibid., 200.

14. References to *Swarm* are by lettered act and numbered scene.

15. Müller's late performance piece *Mommsen's Block* (available in English in *Drama Contemporary: Germany,* ed. Carl Weber [Baltimore: Johns Hopkins University Press, 1994], 265–76) is dedicated to Guattari. Negri recalls studying Müller's work with Guattari in Paris in "L'impunito' e l'eterno," in *Heiner Müller: Per un teatro pieno di tempo,* ed. Francesco Fiorentino (Rome: Artemide, 2005), 51–53.

16. Negri, "L'impunito' e l'eterno," 52.

17. Ibid., 53.

18. Negri, personal correspondence with the translator.

19. Hardt and Negri, *Multitude,* 344–45.

20. In the script, the protagonist is called simply "Man," but in Nicolier's productions the role was played alternately by the actress Évelyne Didi and by a group of male and female Sorbonne students, so for convenience I will refer to the protagonist as "she."

21. References to *The Bent Man* and *Cithaeron* are by numbered act and lettered or named scene.

22. Michael Hardt and Antonio Negri, *Empire* (Cambridge: Harvard University Press, 2000), 212.

23. Hardt and Negri, *Multitude,* 342.

24. Antonio Negri, *Books for Burning: Between Civil War and Democracy in 1970s Italy,* ed. Timothy S. Murphy, trans. Arianna Bove, Ed Emery, Timothy S. Murphy, and Francesco Novello (New York: Verso, 2005), 259.

25. Perhaps the reverberation of this passage that is most relevant to my argument here is its citation in the libretto of a recent music-theater piece composed by the contrabassist Stefano Scodanibbio in 2004 and staged

in collaboration with Giorgio Agamben and the painter Gianni Dessi in Stuttgart and Tolentino in 2006. Scodanibbio worked closely with Luigi Nono during the 1970s and 1980s, and his "music drama" *Il cielo sulla terra* (*The Sky Fallen to Earth* or *Heaven on Earth*) is a nonnarrative, multimedia meditation on the Italian counterculture of the 1970s and its precursors (the Beats, the Berkeley Free Speech Movement, May '68 in Paris) that owes a clear debt to Nono's stage works. Its opening scene is a constellation of media images from the period, followed by a scene of dancing children who construct a cityscape out of old books. In the next scene, this new world darkens before being invaded by sirens and searchlights as Negri himself reads the ski mask passage from offstage to mark the transition from the period of the counterculture's expansion and intensification to that of its criminalization and suppression. Later scenes cite other influential figures of the global counterculture, from Kerouac, Burroughs, and Debord to Deleuze and Guattari, but only Negri's words are heard as part of the soundscape, and only they are used to mark a shift that is simultaneously historical and aesthetic. I suspect that this theatrical experience is somehow related to Negri's own turn to the theater.

26. Aristotle, *Poetics,* in *Basic Works of Aristotle,* ed. Richard McKeon, trans. Ingram Bywater (New York: Random House, 1941), 1459.

27. Bertolt Brecht, *The Measures Taken,* in *The Jewish Wife and Other Plays,* ed. and trans. Eric Bentley (New York: Grove Press, 1965), 75–108.

28. Heiner Müller, *Mauser,* in *The Battle: Plays, Prose, Poems,* ed. and trans. Carl Weber (New York: Performing Arts Journal, 1989), 117–34.

29. In one version of the Paris stage production, actress Didi played both the protagonist and the chorus (the latter appearing in the form of her amplified voice). In the other version, both the protagonist and the chorus were played by groups of Sorbonne students, who recited the dialogue slightly out of unison in an attempt to put the multitude or swarm onstage as literally as possible.

30. Hardt and Negri, *Empire,* 413.

31. Hardt and Negri, *Multitude,* 92.

32. Ibid., 339.

33. Ibid., 341–42.

34. Ibid., 346–47.

35. In this it is formally and substantially prefigured by the "dialogue between a prisoner and a free man" that constitutes Negri's preface to the English-language edition of *Marx beyond Marx* (Brooklyn: Autonomedia, 1991), xiv–xvii.

36. Hardt and Negri, *Multitude,* 344–45.

37. Like one version of her production of *Swarm,* Nicolier's production of

Cithaeron cast groups of Sorbonne students in each of the individual roles.

38. Michael Hardt and Antonio Negri, *Labor of Dionysus: A Critique of the State-Form* (Minneapolis: University of Minnesota Press, 1994), xiii–xiv.

39. See Michael Hardt, "Into the Factory: Negri's Lenin and the Subjective Caesura (1968–73)," in *The Philosophy of Antonio Negri: Resistance in Practice,* ed. Timothy S. Murphy and Abdul-Karim Mustapha (London: Pluto Press, 2005), 7–37.

40. See Gilles Deleuze and Michel Foucault, "Intellectuals and Power," in Michel Foucault, *Language, Counter-Memory, Practice,* ed. Donald F. Bouchard (Ithaca, N.Y.: Cornell University Press, 1977), 205–7.

41. Hardt and Negri, *Multitude,* 210–11.

42. Ibid., 339.

Swarm

1. At the premiere of this play in 2005 at the Théâtre de Vidy-Lausanne, the director Barbara Nicolier, after discussions with the author, inserted excerpts from Charlotte Beradt's *The Third Reich of Dreams* before the start of this first scene.

2. Cf. Antonio Gramsci in the *Prison Notebooks:* "the old is dying and the new cannot be born: in this interregnum, morbid phenomena of the most varied kind come to pass" (*Prison Notebooks,* vol. 2, ed. and trans. Joseph Buttigieg [New York: Columbia University Press, 1992], 33).

3. Heiner Müller, *The Task* (1979), in *Hamletmachine and Other Texts for the Stage,* trans. Carl Weber (modified) (New York: Performing Arts Journal, 1984), 87.

4. See Walter Benjamin, thesis IX in "Theses on the Philosophy of History," in *Illuminations,* trans. Harry Zohn (New York: Schocken, 1969), 257–58.

5. Cf. Mao Tse-tung, "A Single Spark Can Start a Prairie Fire," in *Selected Works,* vol. 1 (Peking: Foreign Languages Press, 1965), 117–28.

The Bent Man

1. Samuel Beckett, *Endgame* (1958), in Samuel Beckett, *The Grove Centenary Edition Volume III: Dramatic Works* (New York: Grove Press, 2006), 104.

2. Ibid., 98.

ANTONIO NEGRI is an independent scholar and political activist. He taught political science at the University of Paris and the University of Padua and is the author of more than thirty books, many of which have been translated into several languages. Among his translated works in English are *The Savage Anomaly* (Minnesota, 1991); *Marx beyond Marx*; *Insurgencies: Constituent Power and the Modern State* (Minnesota, 1999, 2009); *Time for Revolution*; and *Books for Burning*. He is coauthor, with Michael Hardt, of *Labor of Dionysus: A Critique of the State-Form* (Minnesota, 1994) and, with Cesare Casarino, of *In Praise of the Common: A Conversation on Philosophy and Politics* (Minnesota, 2008). He was the most prominent figure in the Autonomia movement in Italy in the 1970s, and he has participated several times in the Global Social Forum. Many of his works have inspired contemporary antiglobalization political movements around the world.

TIMOTHY S. MURPHY is associate professor of English at the University of Oklahoma. He edits the journal *Genre: Forms of Discourse and Culture* and is author of *Wising Up the Marks: The Amodern William Burroughs*; editor of *The Philosophy of Antonio Negri*, volumes 1 and 2; and translator of Negri's *Subversive Spinoza* and *Books for Burning*.

BARBARA NICOLIER is a director living in Paris. She works on contemporary drama at Théâtre de Vidy-Lausanne and Théâtre National de la Colline in Paris and at the Schauspielhaus in Salzburg. She premiered many of Negri's plays for the stage and performed *Trilogie de la différence* for a French radio broadcast.